ON THE HISTORY OF THE PSYCHO-ANALYTIC MOVEMENT

By Sigmund Freud

On the History of the Psycho-Analytic Movement

SIGMUND FREUD

Translation by
JOAN RIVIERE

Revised and edited,
with a sketch of Freud's life and
ideas and a chronological table, by
JAMES STRACHEY

The Norton Library
W · W · NORTON & COMPANY · INC ·
NEW YORK

FIRST PUBLISHED IN THE NORTON LIBRARY 1967

W. W. Norton & Company, Inc. is also the publisher of
the works of Erik H. Erikson, Otto Fenichel, Karen Horney and
Harry Stack Sullivan, and the principal works of Sigmund Freud.

PRINTED IN THE UNITED STATES OF AMERICA

1 2 3 4 5 6 7 8 9 0

CONTENTS

SIGMUND FREUD

A SKETCH OF HIS LIFE AND IDEAS

Sigmund Freud was born on 6 May 1856 in Freiberg, a small town in Moravia, which was at that time a part of Austria-Hungary. In an external sense the eighty-three years of his life were on the whole uneventful and call for no lengthy history.

He came of a middle-class Jewish family and was the eldest child of his father's second wife. His position in the family was a little unusual, for there were already two grown-up sons by his father's first wife. They were more than twenty years older than he was and one of them was already married, with a little boy; so that Freud was in fact born an uncle. This nephew played at least as important a part in his very earliest years as his own younger brothers and sisters, of whom seven were born after him.

His father was a wool-merchant and soon after Freud's birth found himself in increasing commercial difficulties. He therefore decided, when Freud was just three years old, to leave Freiberg, and a year later the whole family settled in Vienna, with the exception of the two elder half-brothers and their children, who established themselves instead in Manchester. At more than one stage in his life Freud played with the idea of joining them in England, but nothing was to come of this for nearly eighty years.

In Vienna during the whole of Freud's childhood the family lived in the most straitened conditions; but it is much to his father's credit that he gave invariable priority to the charge of Freud's education, for the boy was obviously intelligent and was a hard worker as well. The result was that he won a place in the 'Gymnasium' at the early age of nine, and for the six of the eight years he spent at the school he was regularly top of his class. When at the age of seventeen he passed out of school his career was still undecided; his education so far had been of the most general kind, and, though he seemed in any case destined for the University, several faculties lay open to him.

Freud insisted more than once that at no time in his life did he feel 'any particular predilection for the career of a doctor. I was moved, rather', he says, 'by a sort of curiosity, which was, however, directed more towards human concerns than towards natural objects.' Elsewhere he writes: 'I have no knowledge of having had any craving in my early childhood to help suffering humanity. . . . In my youth I felt an overpowering need to understand something of the riddles of the world in which we live and perhaps even to contribute something to their solution.' And in yet another passage in which he was discussing the sociological studies of his last years: 'My interest, after making a lifelong *détour* through the natural sciences, medicine, and psychotherapy, returned to the cultural problems which had fascinated me long before, when I was a youth scarcely old enough for thinking.'

What immediately determined Freud's choice of a scientific career was, so he tells us, being present just when he was leaving school at a public reading of an extremely flowery essay on 'Nature', attributed (wrongly, it seems) to Goethe. But if it was to be science, practical considerations narrowed the choice to medicine. And it was as a medical student that Freud enrolled himself at the University in the autumn of 1873 at the age of seventeen. Even so, however, he was in no hurry to obtain a medical degree. For his first year or two he attended lectures on a variety of subjects, but gradually concentrated first on biology and then on physiology. His very first piece of research was in his third year at the University, when he was deputed by the Professor of Comparative Anatomy to investigate a detail in the anatomy of the eel, which involved the dissection of some four hundred specimens. Soon afterwards he entered the Physiological Laboratory under Brücke, and worked there happily for six years. It was no doubt from him that he acquired the main outlines of his attitude to physical science in general. During these years Freud worked chiefly on the anatomy of the central nervous system and was already beginning to produce publications. But it was becoming obvious that no livelihood which would be sufficient to meet the needs of the large family at home was to be picked up from these laboratory studies. So at last, in 1881, he decided to take his medical degree, and a year later, most unwillingly, gave up his position under Brücke and began work in the Vienna General Hospital.

What finally determined this change in his life was something more urgent than family considerations: in June 1882 he became engaged to be married, and thenceforward all his efforts were directed towards making marriage possible. His fiancée, Martha Bernays, came of a well-known Jewish family in Hamburg, and though for the moment she was living in Vienna she was very soon obliged to return to her remote North-German home. During the four years that followed, it was only for brief visits that he could have glimpses of her, and the two lovers had to content themselves with an almost daily interchange of letters. Freud now set himself to establishing a position and a reputation in the medical world. He worked in various departments of the hospital, but soon came to concentrate on neuro-anatomy and neuro-pathology. During this period, too, he published the first inquiry into the possible medical uses of cocaine; and it was this that suggested to Koller the drug's employment as a local anaesthetic. He soon formed two immediate plans: one of these was to obtain an appointment as *Privatdozent,* a post not unlike that of a university lecturer in England, the other was to gain a travelling bursary which would enable him to spend some time in Paris where the reigning figure was the great Charcot. Both of these aims, if they were realized, would, he felt, bring him real advantages, and in 1885, after a hard struggle, he achieved them both.

The months which Freud spent under Charcot at the Salpêtrière (the famous Paris hospital for nervous diseases) brought another change in the course of his life and this time a revolutionary one. So far his work had been concerned entirely with physical science and he was still carrying out histological studies on the brain while he was in Paris. Charcot's interests were at that period concentrated mainly on hysteria and hypnotism. In the world from which Freud came these subjects were regarded as barely respectable, but he became absorbed in them, and, though Charcot himself looked at them purely as branches of neuropathology, for Freud they meant the first beginning of the investigation of the mind.

On his return to Vienna in the spring of 1886 Freud set up in private practice as a consultant in nervous diseases, and his long-delayed marriage followed soon afterwards. He did not, however, at once abandon all his neuropathological work: for several years he studied in particular the cerebral palsies of children, on which he became a leading authority. At this period, too, he produced an important monograph on aphasia. But he was becoming more and more engaged in the treatment of the neuroses. After experimenting in vain with electro-therapy, he turned to hypnotic sug-

gestion, and in 1888 visited Nancy to learn the technique used
with such apparent success there by Liébeault and Bernheim.
This still proved unsatisfactory and he was driven to yet another
line of approach. He knew that a friend of his, Dr. Josef Breuer,
a Vienna consultant considerably his senior, had some ten years
earlier cured a girl suffering from hysteria by a quite new procedure. He now persuaded Breuer to take up the method once
more, and he himself applied it to several fresh cases with promising results. The method was based on the assumption that
hysteria was the product of a psychical trauma which had been
forgotten by the patient; and the treatment consisted in inducing
her in a hypnotic state to recall the forgotten trauma to the ac-
companiment of appropriate emotions. Before very long Freud
began to make changes both in the procedure and in the underlying theory; this led eventually to a breach with Breuer, and to
the ultimate development by Freud of the whole system of ideas
to which he soon gave the name of psycho-analysis.

From this moment onwards—from 1895, perhaps—to the very
end of his life, the whole of Freud's intellectual existence revolved
around this development, its far-reaching implications, and its
theoretical and practical repercussions. It would, of course, be impossible to give in a few sentences any consecutive account of
Freud's discoveries and ideas, but an attempt will be made pres-
ently to indicate in a disconnected fashion some of the main
changes he has brought about in our habits of thought. Meanwhile we may continue to follow the course of his external life.

His domestic existence in Vienna was essentially devoid of
episode: his home and his consulting rooms were in the same
house from 1891 till his departure for London forty-seven years
later. His happy marriage and his growing family—three sons and
three daughters—provided a solid counterweight to the difficulties
which, to begin with at least, surrounded his professional career.
It was not only the nature of his discoveries that created prejudice
against him in medical circles; just as great, perhaps, was the effect
of the intense anti-semitic feeling which dominated the official
world of Vienna: his appointment to a university professorship
was constantly held back by political influence.

One particular feature of these early years calls for mention on
account of its consequences. This was Freud's friendship with
Wilhelm Fliess, a brilliant but unbalanced Berlin physician, who
specialized in the ear and throat, but whose wider interests ex-

tended over human biology and the effects of periodic phenomena in vital processes. For fifteen years, from 1887 to 1902, Freud corresponded with him regularly, reported the development of his ideas, forwarded him long drafts outlining his future writings, and, most important of all, sent him an essay of some forty thousand words which has been given the name of a 'Project for a Scientific Psychology'. This essay was composed in 1895, at what might be described as the water-shed of Freud's career, when he was reluctantly moving from physiology to psychology; it is an attempt to state the facts of psychology in purely neurological terms. This paper and all the rest of Freud's communications to Fliess have, by a lucky chance, survived: they throw a fascinating light on the development of Freud's ideas and show how much of the later findings of psycho-analysis were already present in his mind at this early stage.

Apart from his relations with Fliess, Freud had little outside support to begin with. He gradually gathered a few pupils round him in Vienna, but it was only after some ten years, in about 1906, that a change was inaugurated by the adhesion of a number of Swiss psychiatrists to his views. Chief among these were Bleuler, the head of the Zürich mental hospital, and his assistant Jung. This proved to be the beginning of the first spread of psycho-analysis. An international meeting of psycho-analysts gathered at Salzburg in 1908, and in 1909 Freud and Jung were invited to give a number of lectures in the United States. Freud's writings began to be translated into many languages, and groups of practising analysts sprang up all over the world. But the progress of psycho-analysis was not without its set-backs: the currents which its subject-matter stirred up in the mind ran too deep for its easy acceptance. In 1911 one of Freud's prominent Viennese supporters, Alfred Adler, broke away from him, and two or three years later Jung's differences from Freud led to their separation. Almost immediately after this came the First World War and an interruption of the international spread of psycho-analysis. Soon afterwards, too, came the gravest personal tragedies—the death of a daughter and of a favourite grandchild, and the onset of the malignant illness which was to pursue him relentlessly for the last sixteen years of his life. None of these troubles, however, brought any interruption to the development of Freud's observations and inferences. The structure of his ideas continued to expand and to find ever wider applications—particularly in the sociological field.

By now he had become generally recognized as a figure of world celebrity, and no honour pleased him more than his election in 1936, the year of his eightieth birthday, as a Corresponding Member of the Royal Society. It was no doubt this fame, supported by the efforts of influential admirers, including, it is said, President Roosevelt, that protected him from the worst excesses of the National Socialists when Hitler invaded Austria in 1938, though they seized and destroyed his publications. Freud's departure from Vienna was nevertheless essential, and in June of that year, accompanied by some of his family, he made the journey to London, and it was there, a year later, on 23 September 1939, that he died.

It has become a journalistic cliché to speak of Freud as one of the revolutionary founders of modern thought and to couple his name with that of Einstein. Most people would however find it almost as hard to summarize the changes introduced by the one as by the other.

Freud's discoveries may be grouped under three headings—an instrument of research, the findings produced by the instrument, and the theoretical hypotheses inferred from the findings—though the three groups were of course mutually interrelated. Behind all of Freud's work, however, we should posit his belief in the universal validity of the law of determinism. As regards physical phenomena this belief was perhaps derived from his experience in Brücke's laboratory and so, ultimately, from the school of Helmholz; but Freud extended the belief uncompromisingly to the field of mental phenomena, and here he may have been influenced by his teacher, the psychiatrist Meynert, and indirectly by the philosophy of Herbart.

First and foremost, Freud was the discoverer of the first instrument for the scientific examination of the human mind. Creative writers of genius had had fragmentary insight into mental processes, but no systematic method of investigation existed before Freud. It was only gradually that he perfected the instrument, since it was only gradually that the difficulties in the way of such an investigation became apparent. The forgotten trauma in Breuer's explanation of hysteria provided the earliest problem and perhaps the most fundamental of all, for it showed conclusively that there were active parts of the mind not immediately open to inspection either by an onlooker or by the subject himself. These parts of the mind were described by Freud, without regard for metaphysical or terminological disputes, as the unconscious. Their existence was equally demonstrated by the fact of post-hypnotic suggestion, where a person in a fully waking state performs an action which had been suggested to him some time earlier, though he had totally forgotten the suggestion itself. No examination of the mind could thus be considered complete unless it included this unconscious part of it in its scope. How was this to be accomplished? The obvious answer seemed to be: by means of hypnotic suggestion; and this was the instrument used by Breuer and, to begin with, by Freud. But it soon turned out to be an imperfect one, acting irregularly and uncertainly and sometimes not at all. Little by little, accordingly, Freud abandoned the use of suggestion and replaced it by an entirely fresh instrument, which was later known as 'free association'. He adopted the unheard-of plan of simply asking the person whose mind he was investigating to say whatever came into his head. This crucial decision led at once to the most startling results; even in this primitive form Freud's instrument produced fresh insight. For, though things went along swimmingly for a while, sooner or later the flow of associations dried up: the subject would not or could not think of anything more to say. There thus came to light the fact of 'resistance', of a force, separate from the subject's conscious will, which was refusing to collaborate with the investigation. Here was one basis for a very fundamental piece of theory, for a hypothesis of the mind as something dynamic, as consisting in a number of mental forces, some conscious and some unconscious, operating now in harmony now in opposition with one another.

Though these phenomena eventually turned out to be of universal occurrence, they were first observed and studied in neurotic patients, and the earlier years of Freud's work were largely concerned with discovering means by which the 'resistance' of these patients could be overcome and what lay behind it could be brought to light. The solution was only made possible by an extraordinary piece of self-observation on Freud's part—what we should now describe as his self-analysis. We are fortunate in having a contemporary first-hand description of this event in his letters to Fliess which have already been mentioned. This analysis enabled him to discover the nature of the unconscious processes at work in the mind and to understand why there is such a strong resistance to their becoming conscious; it enabled him to devise techniques for overcoming or evading the resistance in his patients; and, most important of all, it enabled him to realize the very great difference between the mode of functioning of these unconscious processes and that of our familiar conscious ones. A word may be said on each of these three points, for in fact they constitute the core of Freud's contributions to our knowledge of the mind.

The unconscious contents of the mind were found to consist wholly in the activity of conative trends—desires or wishes—which derive their energy directly from the primary physical instincts. They function quite regardless of any consideration other than that of obtaining immediate satisfaction, and are thus liable to be out of step with those more conscious elements in the mind which are concerned with adaptation to reality and the avoidance of external dangers. Since, moreover, these primitive trends are to a great extent of a sexual or of a destructive nature, they are bound to come in conflict with the more social and civilized mental forces. Investigations along this path were what led Freud to his discoveries of the long-disguised secrets of the sexual life of children and of the Oedipus complex.

In the second place, his self-analysis led him to an inquiry into the nature of dreams. These turned out to be, like neurotic symptoms, the product of a conflict and a compromise between the primary unconscious impulses and the secondary conscious ones. By analysing them into their elements it was therefore possible to infer their hidden unconscious contents; and, since dreams are common phenomena of almost universal occurrence, their interpretation turned out to be one of the most useful technical contrivances for penetrating the resistances of neurotic patients.

Finally, the painstaking examination of dreams enabled Freud to classify the remarkable differences between what he termed the primary and secondary processes of thought, between events in the unconscious and conscious regions of the mind. In the unconscious, it was found, there is no sort of organization or coordination: each separate impulse seeks satisfaction independently of all the rest; they proceed uninfluenced by one another; contradictions are completely inoperative, and the most opposite impulses flourish side by side. So, too, in the unconscious, associations of ideas proceed along lines without any regard to logic: similarities are treated as identities, negatives are equated with positives. Again, the objects to which the conative trends are attached in the unconscious are extraordinarily changeable—one may be replaced by another along a whole chain of associations that have no rational basis. Freud perceived that the intrusion into conscious thinking of mechanisms that belong properly to the primary process accounts for the oddity not only of dreams but of many other normal and pathological mental events.

It is not much of an exaggeration to say that all the later part of Freud's work lay in an immense extension and elaboration of these early ideas. They were applied to an elucidation of the mechanisms not only of the psychoneuroses and psychoses but also of such normal processes as slips of the tongue, making jokes, artistic creation, political institutions, and religions; they played a part in throwing fresh light on many applied sciences—archaeology, anthropology, criminology, education; they also served to account for the effectiveness of psycho-analytic therapy. Lastly, too, Freud erected on the basis of these elementary observations a theoretical superstructure, what he named a 'metapsychology', of more general concepts. These, however, fascinating as many people will find them, he always insisted were in the nature of provisional hypotheses. Quite late in his life, indeed, influenced by the ambiguity of the term 'unconscious' and its many conflicting uses, he proposed a new structural account of the mind in which the uncoordinated instinctual trends were called the 'id', the organized realistic part the 'ego', and the critical and moralizing function the 'super-ego'—a new account which has certainly made for a clarification of many issues.

This, then, will have given the reader an outline of the external events of Freud's life and some notion of the scope of his discoveries. Is it legitimate to ask for more? to try to penetrate a little further and to inquire what sort of person Freud was? Possibly not. But human curiosity about great men is insatiable, and if it is not gratified with true accounts it will inevitably clutch at mythological ones. In two of Freud's early books (*The Interpretation of Dreams* and *The Psychopathology of Everyday Life*) the presentation of his thesis had forced on him the necessity of bringing up an unusual amount of personal material. Nevertheless, or perhaps for that very reason, he intensely objected to any intrusion into his private life, and he was correspondingly the subject of a wealth of myths. According to the first and most naïve rumours, for instance, he was an abandoned profligate, devoted to the corruption of public morals. Later fantasies have tended in the opposite direction: he has been represented as a harsh moralist, a ruthless disciplinarian, an autocrat, egocentric and unsmiling, and an essentially unhappy man. To anyone who was acquainted with him, even slightly, both these pictures must seem equally preposterous. The second of them was no doubt partly derived from a knowledge of his physical sufferings during his last years; but partly too it may have been due to the unfortunate impression produced by some of his most widespread portraits. He disliked being photographed, at least by professional photographers, and his features on occasion expressed the fact; artists too seem always to have been overwhelmed by the necessity for representing the inventor of psycho-analysis as a ferocious and terrifying figure. Fortunately, however, alternative versions exist of a more amiable and truer kind—snapshots, for instance, taken on a holiday or with his children, such as will be found in his eldest son's memoir of his father (*Glory Reflected,* by Martin Freud). In many ways, indeed, this delightful and amusing book serves to redress the balance from more official biographies. invaluable as they are, and reveals something of Freud as he was in ordinary life. Some of these portraits show us that in his earlier days he had well-filled features, but in later life, at any rate after the First World War and even before his illness, this was no longer so, and his features, as well as his whole figure (which was of medium height), were chiefly remarkable for the impression they gave of tense energy and alert observation. He was serious but kindly and considerate in his more formal manners, but in other circumstances could be an entertaining talker with a pleasantly ironical sense of humour. It was easy to discover his devoted fondness for his family and to recognize a man who would inspire affection. He had many miscellaneous interests—he was fond of travelling abroad, of country holidays, of mountain walks—and there were other, more engrossing subjects, art, archaeology, literature. Freud was a very well-read man in many languages, not only in German. He read English and French fluently, besides having a fair knowledge of Spanish and Italian. It must be remembered, too, that though the later phases of his education were chiefly scientific (it is true that at the University he studied philosophy for a short time) at school he had learnt the classics and never lost his affection for them. We happen to have a letter written by him at the age of seventeen to a school friend. In it he describes his varying success in the different papers of his school-leaving examination:

in Latin a passage from Virgil, and in Greek thirty-three lines from, of all things, *Oedipus Rex*.

In short, we might regard Freud as what in England we should consider the best kind of product of a Victorian upbringing. His tastes in literature and art would obviously differ from ours, his views on ethics, though decidedly liberal, would not belong to the post-Freudian age. But we should see in him a man who lived a life of full emotion and of much suffering without embitterment. Complete honesty and directness were qualities that stood out in him, and so too did his intellectual readiness to take in and consider any fact, however new or extraordinary, that was presented to him. It was perhaps an inevitable corollary and extension of these qualities, combined with a general benevolence which a surface misanthropy failed to disguise, that led to some features of a surprising kind. In spite of his subtlety of mind he was essentially unsophisticated, and there were sometimes unexpected lapses in his critical faculty—a failure, for instance, to perceive an untrustworthy authority in some subject that was off his own beat such as Egyptology or philology, and, strangest of all in someone whose powers of perception had to be experienced to be believed, an occasional blindness to defects in his acquaintances. But though it may flatter our vanity to declare that Freud was a human being of a kind like our own, that satisfaction can easily be carried too far. There must in fact have been something very extraordinary in the man who was first able to recognize a whole field of mental facts which had hitherto been excluded from normal consciousness, the man who first interpreted dreams, who first accepted the facts of infantile sexuality, who first made the distinction between the primary and secondary processes of thinking—the man who first made the unconscious mind real to us.

JAMES STRACHEY

Those in search of further information will find it in Ernest Jones's biography of Freud, in the collection of his letters edited by his son, Ernst Freud, and in the many volumes of the Standard Edition of his complete psychological works.

CHRONOLOGICAL TABLE

This table traces very roughly some of the main turning-points in Freud's intellectual development and opinions. A few of the chief events in his external life are also included in it.

1856. 6 May. Birth at Freiberg in Moravia.

1860. Family settles in Vienna.

1865. Enters Gymnasium (secondary school).

1873. Enters Vienna University as medical student.

1876–82. Works under Brücke at the Institute of Physiology in Vienna.

1877. First publications: papers on anatomy and physiology.

1881. Graduates as Doctor of Medicine.

1882. Engagement to Martha Bernays.

1882–5. Works in Vienna General Hospital, concentrating on cerebral anatomy: numerous publications.

1884–7. Researches into the clinical uses of cocaine.

1885. Appointed *Privatdozent* (University Lecturer) in Neuropathology.

1885 (October)–1886 (February). Studies under Charcot at the Salpêtrière (hospital for nervous diseases) in Paris. Interest first turns to hysteria and hypnosis.

1886. Marriage to Martha Bernays. Sets up private practice in nervous diseases in Vienna.

1886–93. Continues work on neurology, especially on the cerebral palsies of children at the Kassowitz Institute in Vienna, with numerous publications. Gradual shift of interest from neurology to psychopathology.

1887. Birth of eldest child (Mathilde).

1887–1902. Friendship and correspondence with Wilhelm Fliess in Berlin. Freud's letters to him during this period, published posthumously in 1950, throw much light on the development of his views.

1887. Begins the use of hypnotic suggestion in his practice.

c. 1888. Begins to follow Breuer in using hypnosis for cathartic treatment of hysteria. Gradually drops hypnosis and substitutes free association.

1889. Visits Bernheim at Nancy to study his suggestion technique.

1889. Birth of eldest son (Martin).

1891. Monograph on aphasia.

Birth of second son (Oliver).

1892. Birth of youngest son (Ernst).

1893. Publication of Breuer and Freud 'Preliminary Communication': exposition of trauma theory of hysteria and of cathartic treatment.

Birth of second daughter (Sophie).

1893–8. Researches and short papers on hysteria, obsessions, and anxiety.

1895. Jointly with Breuer, *Studies on Hysteria*: case histories and description by Freud of his technique, including first account of transference.

1893–6. Gradual divergence of views between Freud and Breuer. Freud introduces concepts of defence and repression and of neurosis being a result of a conflict between the ego and the libido.

1895. *Project for a Scientific Psychology*: included in Freud's letters to Fliess and first published in 1950. An abortive attempt to state psychology in neurological terms; but foreshadows much of Freud's later theories.

Birth of youngest child (Anna).

1896. Introduces the term 'psycho-analysis'.

Death of father (aged 80).

1897. Freud's self-analysis, leading to the abandonment of the trauma theory and the recognition of infantile sexuality and the Oedipus complex.

1900. *The Interpretation of Dreams*, with final chapter giving first full account of Freud's dynamic view of mental processes, of the unconscious, and of the dominance of the 'pleasure principle'.

1901. *The Psychopathology of Everyday Life*. This, together with the book on dreams, made it plain that Freud's theories applied not only to pathological states but also to normal mental life.

1902. Appointed Professor Extraordinarius.

1905. *Three Essays on the Theory of Sexuality*: tracing for the first time the course of development of the sexual instinct in human beings from infancy to maturity.

c. 1906. Jung becomes an adherent of psycho-analysis.

1908. First international meeting of psycho-analysts (at Salzburg).

1909. Freud and Jung invited to the U.S.A. to lecture.

Case history of the first analysis of a child (Little Hans, aged five): confirming inference previously made from adult analyses, especially as to infantile sexuality and the Oedipus and castration complexes.

c. 1910. First emergence of the theory of 'narcissism'.

1911–15. Papers on the technique of psycho-analysis.

1911. Secession of Adler.

Application of psycho-analytic theories to a psychotic case: the autobiography of Dr. Schreber.

1913–14. *Totem and Taboo*: application of psycho-analysis to anthropological material.

1914. Secession of Jung.

'On the History of the Psycho-Analytic Movement'. Includes a polemical section on Adler and Jung.

Writes his last major case history, of the 'Wolf Man' (not published till 1918).

1915. Writes a series of twelve 'metapsychological' papers on basic theoretical questions, of which only five have survived.

1915–17. *Introductory Lectures*: giving an extensive general account of the state of Freud's views up to the time of the First World War.

1919. Application of the theory of narcissism to the war neuroses.

1920. Death of second daughter.

Beyond the Pleasure Principle; the first explicit introduction of the concept of the 'compulsion to repeat' and of the theory of the 'death instinct'.

1921. *Group Psychology*. Beginnings of a systematic analytic study of the ego.

1923. *The Ego and the Id*. Largely revised account of the structure and functioning of the mind with the division into an id, an ego, and a super-ego.

1923. First onset of cancer.

1925. Revised views on the sexual development of women.

1926. *Inhibitions, Symptoms, and Anxiety*. Revised views on the problem of anxiety.

1927. *The Future of an Illusion*. A discussion of religion: the first of a number of sociological works to which Freud devoted most of his remaining years.

1930. *Civilization and its Discontents*. This includes Freud's first extensive study of the destructive instinct (regarded as a manifestation of the 'death instinct').

Freud awarded the Goethe Prize by the City of Frankfurt.

Death of mother (aged 95).

1933. Hitler seizes power in Germany: Freud's books publicly burned in Berlin.

1934–8. *Moses and Monotheism*: the last of Freud's works to appear during his lifetime.

1936. Eightieth birthday. Election as Corresponding Member of Royal Society.

1938. Hitler's invasion of Austria. Freud leaves Vienna for London.

An Outline of Psycho-analysis. A final, unfinished, but profound, exposition of psycho-analysis.

1939. 23 September. Death in London.

ON THE HISTORY OF THE PSYCHO-ANALYTIC MOVEMENT

.

EDITOR'S NOTE

This work was written by Freud during January and February, 1914. The preceding period had been one of strain and conflict among his early followers. Adler's disagreements with the views of Freud had come to a head in 1910, and Jung's some three years later. The detailed story of these difficulties will be found in Chapter V of the second volume of Ernest Jones's Freud biography, and a contemporary account of them may be followed in the correspondence between Freud and Karl Abraham. In spite, however, of the wide divergences separating Adler and Jung from Freud, they had persisted in describing their theories as 'psycho-analysis.'

Freud's immediate aim in writing the present work was to state as clearly as possible the fundamental postulates and hypotheses of psycho-analysis, to show that the theories of Adler and Jung were totally incompatible with them, and to draw the inference that it would lead to nothing but general confusion if these contradictory sets of views were all given the same name. Freud's argument was partially effective. Adler had already chosen the name of 'Individual Psychology' for his theories, and soon afterwards Jung adopted that of 'Analytical Psychology.' Nevertheless, popular opinion continued for many years to insist that there were 'three schools of psycho-analysis'; and to this very day uninstructed critics are to be found who are eager to include the names of Freud, Adler, and Jung in a single bracket. Thus the value of the present essay in clarification is far from exhausted.

In order to make the essential principles of psycho-analysis perfectly plain, Freud traced the history of their development from their pre-analytic beginnings. The first section of the work covers the period during which he himself was the only person concerned — that is, up till about 1902. The second section takes the story on till about 1910 — the time during which psycho-analytic views first began to extend to wider circles. It is only in the third section that Freud comes to a discussion of the dissident views, first of Adler and then of Jung, and points out the vital respects in which they depart from the findings of psycho-analysis.

In this last section, and also to some extent in the whole of the work, we find Freud adopting a much more belligerent tone than in any other of his controversial writings whether earlier or later. Other works of the same period bear witness to the feelings stirred in him by these defections. Some paragraphs, for instance, in Section I of the almost contemporary paper 'Narcissim' (1914c) are devoted to criticisms of Jung, and a similar passage dealing with Adler appears at the beginning of Section III of the same paper. So too the important case history of the 'Wolf Man,' which was mainly written in the same year though not published until 1918, was largely designed as an empirical refutation of Adler and Jung and contains many attacks on their theories.

In Freud's later works references to these controversies rapidly diminish in number and become drier in tone. The modern reader may be surprised at the remark (on page 60) that 'of the two movements under discussion Adler's is indubitably the more important.' But there is plenty of other evidence that this was Freud's considered opinion. Thus there is a long and closely reasoned discussion of Adler's views on the motive forces leading to repression in the final section of Freud's paper on beating-phantasies (1919e) . And in Lecture XXXIV of *New Introductory Lectures* (1933a) (Norton, 1965) , written towards the end of Freud's life, there are several pages of severe criticism of Adler, whereas the name of Jung does not so much as appear in those lectures.

Some ten years after writing the present work Freud went over much of the same historical ground in *An Autobiographical Study* (1925d) . But his mood was by then very different and the controversies which had engendered so much bitterness had faded into the background.

The first German edition of this work appeared in a

periodical (*Jahrbuch der Psychoanalyse*) in 1914. It was first published in volume form in 1924, when a very few minor alterations were made and a long footnote (page 33-34 below) was added. The first English translation, by A. A. Brill, came out in 1916. A new one, by Joan Riviere, was included in Volume I of Freud's *Collected Papers* in 1924. A considerably modified version of the latter was taken over in Volume XIV of the *Standard Edition* of Freud's works, and, with some very slight changes, this modified version is reprinted here.

JAMES STRACHEY

ON THE HISTORY OF THE PSYCHO-ANALYTIC MOVEMENT

Fluctuat nec mergitur
(On the coat of arms of the City of Paris [1])

I

No one need be surprised at the subjective character of the contribution I propose to make here to the history of the psycho-analytic movement, nor need anyone wonder at the part I play in it. For psycho-analysis is my creation; for ten years I was the only person who concerned himself with it, and all the dissatisfaction which the new phenomenon aroused in my contemporaries has been poured out in the form of criticisms on my head. Although it is a long time now since I was the only psycho-analyst, I consider myself justified in maintaining that even to-day no one can know better than I do what psycho-analysis is, how it differs from other ways of investigating the life of the mind, and precisely what should be called psycho-analysis and what would better be described by some other name. In thus repudiating what seems to me a cool act of usurpation, I am indirectly informing the readers of this *Jahrbuch* of the events that have led to the changes in its editorship and format. [2]

In 1909, in the lecture-room of an American university, I had my first opportunity of speaking in public about psychoanalysis. [3] The occasion was a momentous one for my work, and moved by this thought I then declared that it was not I who had

[1] [The coat of arms represents a ship, and the device may be rendered 'it is tossed by the waves, but does not sink'. Freud quoted the motto twice in his correspondence with Fliess, in connection with his own state of mind (Letters 119 and 143, Freud, 1950*a*).]

[2] [The *Jahrbuch* had hitherto been under the direction of Bleuler and Freud and edited by Jung. Freud himself now became sole director and the editorship was taken over by Abraham and Hitschmann. Cf. also p. 46 below.]

[3] In my 'Five Lectures' (1910*a*), delivered at Clark University. [See below, pp. 30–1.]

7

brought psycho-analysis into existence: the credit for this was due to someone else, to Josef Breuer, whose work had been done at a time when I was still a student engaged in passing my examinations (1880–2). Since I gave those lectures, however, some well-disposed friends have suggested to me a doubt whether my gratitude was not expressed too extravagantly on that occasion. In their view I ought to have done as I had previously been accustomed to do: treated Breuer's 'cathartic procedure' as a preliminary stage of psycho-analysis, and represented psycho-analysis itself as beginning with my discarding the hypnotic technique and introducing free associations. It is of no great importance in any case whether the history of psycho-analysis is reckoned as beginning with the cathartic method or with my modification of it; I refer to this uninteresting point merely because certain opponents of psycho-analysis have a habit of occasionally recollecting that after all the art of psycho-analysis was not invented by me, but by Breuer. This only happens, of course, if their views allow them to find something in it deserving attention; if they set no such limits to their rejection of it, psycho-analysis is always without question my work alone. I have never heard that Breuer's great share in psycho-analysis has earned him a proportionate measure of criticism and abuse. As I have long recognized that to stir up contradiction and arouse bitterness is the inevitable fate of psycho-analysis, I have come to the conclusion that I must be the true originator of all that is particularly characteristic in it. I am happy to be able to add that none of the efforts to minimize my part in creating this much-abused analysis have ever come from Breuer himself or could claim any support from him.

Breuer's discoveries have so often been described that I can dispense with discussing them in detail here. These were the fundamental fact that the symptoms of hysterical patients are founded upon scenes in their past lives which have made a great impression on them but have been forgotten (traumas); the therapy founded upon this, which consisted in causing them to remember and reproduce these experiences in a state of hypnosis (catharsis); and the fragment of theory inferred from it, which was that these symptoms represented an abnormal employment of amounts of excitation which had not been disposed of (conversion). Whenever Breuer, in his theoretical contribution to the *Studies on Hysteria* (1895), referred to this process of conversion, he always added my name in brackets after it,[1] as though the priority for this first attempt at theoretical evaluation belonged to me. I believe that actually this distinction relates only to the name, and that the conception came to us simultaneously and together.

It is well known, too, that after Breuer made his first discovery of the cathartic method he let it rest for a number of years, and only took it up again at my instigation, on my return from my studies under Charcot.[2] He had a large consulting practice in medicine which made great claims on him; I myself had only unwillingly taken up the profession of medicine, but I had at that time a strong motive for helping people suffering from nervous affections or at least for wishing to understand something about their states. I had embarked upon physical therapy, and had felt absolutely helpless after the disappointing results from my study of Erb's *Elektrotherapie* [1882], which put forward such a number of indications and recommendations. If I did not at the time arrive on my own account at the conclusion which Möbius established later, that the successes of electrical treatment in nervous patients are the effects of suggestion, there is no doubt that only the total absence of these promised successes was to blame. Treatment by suggestion during deep hypnosis, which I learned from Liébeault's and Bernheim's highly impressive demonstrations,[3] then seemed to offer a satisfactory substitute for the failure of electrical treatment. But the practice of *investigating* patients in a state of hypnosis, with which Breuer made me acquainted—a practice which combined an automatic mode of operation with the satisfaction of scientific curiosity—was bound to be incomparably more attractive than the monotonous, forcible prohibitions used in treatment by suggestion, prohibitions which stood in the way of all research.

[1] [There seems to be some mistake here. In the course of Breuer's contribution he uses the term 'conversion' (or its derivatives) at least fifteen times. But only once (the first occasion on which he uses it) does he add Freud's name in brackets. It seems possible that Freud saw some preliminary version of Breuer's manuscript and dissuaded him from adding his name more than once in the printed book. The first published use of the term was before the *Studies on Hysteria*, in Freud's first paper on 'The Neuro-Psychoses of Defence' (1894a).]

[2] [Freud worked at the Salpêtrière in Paris during the winter of 1885–6. See his 'Report on my Studies' (1956a [1886]).]

[3] [Freud spent some weeks at Nancy in 1889.]

We have recently received a piece of advice, purporting to represent one of the latest developments of psycho-analysis, to the effect that the current conflict and the exciting cause of illness are to be brought into the foreground in analysis.[1] Now this is exactly what Breuer and I used to do at the beginning of our work with the cathartic method. We led the patient's attention directly to the traumatic scene in which the symptom had arisen, and we endeavoured to discover the mental conflict in that scene and to release the suppressed affect in it. In the course of this we discovered the mental process, characteristic of the neuroses, which I later named 'regression'. The patient's associations moved back from the scene which we were trying to elucidate to earlier experiences, and compelled the analysis, which was supposed to correct the present, to occupy itself with the past. This regression led constantly further backwards; at first it seemed regularly to bring us to puberty; later on, failures and points which still eluded explanation drew the analytic work still further back into years of childhood which had hitherto been inaccessible to any kind of exploration. This regressive direction became an important characteristic of analysis. It appeared that psycho-analysis could explain nothing belonging to the present without referring back to something past; indeed, that every pathogenic experience implied a previous experience which, though not in itself pathogenic, had yet endowed the later one with its pathogenic quality. The temptation to confine one's attention to the known present exciting cause was so strong, however, that even in later analyses I gave way to it. In the analysis of the patient I named 'Dora' [1905e], carried out in 1899,[2] I had knowledge of the scene which occasioned the outbreak of the current illness. I tried innumerable times to submit this experience to analysis, but even direct demands always failed to produce from her anything more than the same meagre and incomplete description of it. Not until a long détour, leading back over her earliest childhood, had been made, did a dream present itself which on analysis brought to her mind the hitherto forgotten details of this scene, so that a comprehension and a solution of the current conflict became possible.

This one example shows how very misleading is the advice

[1] [Cf. below, p. 63.]
[2] [This is a slip for '1900'.]

referred to above, and what a degree of scientific regression is represented by the neglect of regression in analytic technique which is thus recommended to us.

The first difference between Breuer and myself came to light on a question concerning the finer psychical mechanism of hysteria. He gave preference to a theory which was still to some extent physiological, as one might say; he tried to explain the mental splitting in hysterical patients by the absence of communication between various mental states ('states of consciousness', as we called them at that time), and he therefore constructed the theory of 'hypnoid states', the products of which were supposed to penetrate into 'waking consciousness' like unassimilated foreign bodies. I had taken the matter less scientifically; everywhere I seemed to discern motives and tendencies analogous to those of everyday life, and I looked upon psychical splitting itself as an effect of a process of repelling which at that time I called 'defence', and later, 'repression'.[1] I made a shortlived attempt to allow the two mechanisms a separate existence side by side, but as observation showed me always and only one thing, it was not long before my 'defence' theory took up its stand opposite his 'hypnoid' one.

I am quite sure, however, that this opposition between our views had nothing to do with the breach in our relations which followed shortly after. This had deeper causes, but it came about in such a way that at first I did not understand it; it was only later that I learnt from many clear indications how to interpret it. It will be remembered that Breuer said of his famous first patient that the element of sexuality was astonishingly undeveloped in her [2] and had contributed nothing to the very rich clinical picture of the case. I have always wondered why the critics did not more often cite this assertion of Breuer's as an argument against my contention of a sexual aetiology in the neuroses, and even to-day I do not know whether I ought to regard the omission as evidence of tact or of carelessness on their part. Anyone who reads the history of Breuer's case now in the light of the knowledge gained in the last twenty years will at

[1] [In his *Inhibitions, Symptoms and Anxiety* (1926d). Freud revived the term 'defence' to express a general concept of which 'repression' would denote a sub-species.]

[2] [See the second paragraph of his case history of Anna O. in Breuer and Freud (1895).]

once perceive the symbolism in it—the snakes, the stiffening, the paralysis of the arm—and, on taking into account the situation at the bedside of the young woman's sick father, will easily guess the real interpretation of her symptoms; his opinion of the part played by sexuality in her mental life will therefore be very different from that of her doctor. In his treatment of her case, Breuer was able to make use of a very intense suggestive *rapport* with the patient, which may serve us as a complete prototype of what we call 'transference' to-day. Now I have strong reasons for suspecting that after all her symptoms had been relieved Breuer must have discovered from further indications the sexual motivation of this transference, but that the universal nature of this unexpected phenomenon escaped him, with the result that, as though confronted by an 'untoward event',[1] he broke off all further investigation. He never said this to me in so many words, but he told me enough at different times to justify this reconstruction of what happened. When I later began more and more resolutely to put forward the significance of sexuality in the aetiology of neuroses, he was the first to show the reaction of distaste and repudiation which was later to become so familiar to me, but which at that time I had not yet learnt to recognize as my inevitable fate.[2]

The fact of the emergence of the transference in its crudely sexual form, whether affectionate or hostile, in every treatment of a neurosis, although this is neither desired nor induced by either doctor or patient, has always seemed to me the most irrefragable proof that the source of the driving forces of neurosis lies in sexual life. This argument has never received anything approaching the degree of attention that it merits, for if it had, investigations in this field would leave no other conclusion open. As far as I am concerned, this argument has remained the decisive one, over and above the more specific findings of analytic work.

There was some consolation for the bad reception accorded to my contention of a sexual aetiology in the neuroses even by my more intimate circle of friends—for a vacuum rapidly

[1] [In English in the original. A fuller account of this will be found in the first volume of Ernest Jones's biography (1953, 246 f.).]

[2] [A discussion of Freud's relations with Breuer will be found in the Editor's Introduction to Volume II of the *Standard Edition*.]

formed itself about my person—in the thought that I was taking up the fight for a new and original idea. But, one day, certain memories gathered in my mind which disturbed this pleasing notion, but which gave me in exchange a valuable insight into the processes of human creative activity and the nature of human knowledge. The idea for which I was being made responsible had by no means originated with me. It had been imparted to me by three people whose opinion had commanded my deepest respect—by Breuer himself, by Charcot, and by Chrobak, the gynaecologist at the University, perhaps the most eminent of all our Vienna physicians.[1] These three men had all communicated to me a piece of knowledge which, strictly speaking, they themselves did not possess. Two of them later denied having done so when I reminded them of the fact; the third (the great Charcot) would probably have done the same if it had been granted me to see him again. But these three identical opinions, which I had heard without understanding, had lain dormant in my mind for years, until one day they awoke in the form of an apparently original discovery.

One day, when I was a young house-physician, I was walking across the town with Breuer, when a man came up who evidently wanted to speak to him urgently. I fell behind. As soon as Breuer was free, he told me in his friendly, instructive way that this man was the husband of a patient of his and had brought him some news of her. The wife, he added, was behaving in such a peculiar way in society that she had been brought to him for treatment as a nervous case. He concluded: 'These things are always *secrets d'alcôve*!' I asked him in astonishment what he meant, and he answered by explaining the word *alcôve* ('marriage-bed') to me, for he failed to realize how extraordinary the *matter* of his statement seemed to me.

Some years later, at one of Charcot's evening receptions, I happened to be standing near the great teacher at a moment when he appeared to be telling Brouardel [2] a very interesting

[1] [Rudolf Chrobak (1843–1910) was Professor of Gynaecology at Vienna from 1880–1908.]

[2] [P. C. H. Brouardel (1837–1906) was appointed Professor of Forensic Medicine in Paris in 1879. Freud mentions him appreciatively in his 'Report on my Studies in Paris and Berlin' (1956a [1886]) and also in his preface to Bourke's *Scatalogic Rites of all Nations* (Freud, 1913k).]

story about something that had happened during his day's work. I hardly heard the beginning, but gradually my attention was seized by what he was talking of: a young married couple from a distant country in the East—the woman a severe sufferer, the man either impotent or exceedingly awkward. '*Tâchez donc*,' I heard Charcot repeating, '*je vous assure, vous y arriverez*.'[1] Brouardel, who spoke less loudly, must have expressed his astonishment that symptoms like the wife's could have been produced by such circumstances. For Charcot suddenly broke out with great animation: '*Mais, dans des cas pareils c'est toujours la chose génitale, toujours . . . toujours . . . toujours*';[2] and he crossed his arms over his stomach, hugging himself and jumping up and down on his toes several times in his own characteristically lively way. I know that for a moment I was almost paralysed with amazement and said to myself: 'Well, but if he knows that, why does he never say so?' But the impression was soon forgotten; brain anatomy and the experimental induction of hysterical paralyses absorbed all my interest.

A year later, I had begun my medical career in Vienna as a lecturer in nervous diseases, and in everything relating to the aetiology of the neuroses I was still as ignorant and innocent as one could expect of a promising student trained at a university. One day I had a friendly message from Chrobak, asking me to take a woman patient of his to whom he could not give enough time, owing to his new appointment as a University teacher. I arrived at the patient's house before he did and found that she was suffering from attacks of meaningless anxiety, and could only be soothed by the most precise information about where her doctor was at every moment of the day. When Chrobak arrived he took me aside and told me that the patient's anxiety was due to the fact that although she had been married for eighteen years she was still *virgo intacta*. The husband was absolutely impotent. In such cases, he said, there was nothing for a medical man to do but to shield this domestic misfortune with his own reputation, and put up with it if people shrugged their shoulders and said of him: 'He's no good if he can't cure her after so many years.' The sole prescription for such a

[1] ['Go on trying! I promise you, you'll succeed.']
[2] ['But in this sort of case it's always a question of the genitals—always, always, always.']

malady, he added, is familiar enough to us, but we cannot order it. It runs:

'℞ Penis normalis
dosim
repetatur!'

I had never heard of such a prescription, and felt inclined to shake my head over my kind friend's cynicism.

I have not of course disclosed the illustrious parentage of this scandalous idea in order to saddle other people with the responsibility for it. I am well aware that it is one thing to give utterance to an idea once or twice in the form of a passing *aperçu*, and quite another to mean it seriously—to take it literally and pursue it in the face of every contradictory detail, and to win it a place among accepted truths. It is the difference between a casual flirtation and a legal marriage with all its duties and difficulties. '*Épouser les idées de . . .*' [1] is no uncommon figure of speech, at any rate in French.

Among the other new factors which were added to the cathartic procedure as a result of my work and which transformed it into psycho-analysis, I may mention in particular the theory of repression and resistance, the recognition of infantile sexuality, and the interpreting and exploiting of dreams as a source of knowledge of the unconscious.

The theory of repression quite certainly came to me independently of any other source; I know of no outside impression which might have suggested it to me, and for a long time I imagined it to be entirely original, until Otto Rank (1911*a*) showed us a passage in Schopenhauer's *World as Will and Idea* in which the philosopher seeks to give an explanation of insanity. What he says there about the struggle against accepting a distressing piece of reality coincides with my concept of repression so completely that once again I owe the chance of making a discovery to my not being well-read. Yet others have read the passage and passed it by without making this discovery, and perhaps the same would have happened to me if in my young days I had had more taste for reading philosophical works. In later years I have denied myself the very great pleasure of reading the works of Nietzsche, with the deliberate object of not

[1] ['To espouse an idea.']

being hampered in working out the impressions received in psycho-analysis by any sort of anticipatory ideas. I had therefore to be prepared—and I am so, gladly—to forgo all claims to priority in the many instances in which laborious psychoanalytic investigation can merely confirm the truths which the philosopher recognized by intuition.[1]

The theory of repression is the corner-stone on which the whole structure of psycho-analysis rests. It is the most essential part of it; and yet it is nothing but a theoretical formulation of a phenomenon which may be observed as often as one pleases if one undertakes an analysis of a neurotic without resorting to hypnosis. In such cases one comes across a resistance which opposes the work of analysis and in order to frustrate it pleads a failure of memory. The use of hypnosis was bound to hide this resistance; the history of psycho-analysis proper, therefore, only begins with the new technique that dispenses with hypnosis. The theoretical consideration of the fact that this resistance coincides with an amnesia leads inevitably to the view of unconscious mental activity which is peculiar to psychoanalysis and which, too, distinguishes it quite clearly from philosophical speculations about the unconscious. It may thus be said that the theory of psycho-analysis is an attempt to account for two striking and unexpected facts of observation which emerge whenever an attempt is made to trace the symptoms of a neurotic back to their sources in his past life: the facts of transference and of resistance. Any line of investigation which recognizes these two facts and takes them as the starting-point of its work has a right to call itself psycho-analysis, even though it arrives at results other than my own. But anyone who takes up other sides of the problem while avoiding these two hypotheses will hardly escape a charge of misappropriation of property by attempted impersonation, if he persists in calling himself a psycho-analyst.

If anyone sought to place the theory of repression and resis-

---

[1] [Other instances of the anticipation of Freud's ideas are discussed by him in his 'Note on the Prehistory of the Technique of Analysis' (1920b). See also the remarks on Popper-Lynkeus below (p. 20).—The possibility that Freud derived the term 'repression' indirectly from the early nineteenth-century philosopher Herbart is discussed by Ernest Jones (1953, 407 ff.).]

tance among the *premisses* instead of the *findings* of psycho-analysis, I should oppose him most emphatically. Such premisses of a general psychological and biological nature do exist, and it would be useful to consider them on some other occasion; but the theory of repression is a product of psycho-analytic work, a theoretical inference legitimately drawn from innumerable observations.

Another product of this sort was the hypothesis of infantile sexuality. This, however, was made at a much later date. In the early days of tentative investigation by analysis no such thing was thought of. At first it was merely observed that the effects of present-day experiences had to be traced back to something in the past. But enquirers often find more than they bargain for. One was drawn further and further back into the past; one hoped at last to be able to stop at puberty, the period in which the sexual impulses are traditionally supposed to awake. But in vain; the tracks led still further back into childhood and into its earlier years. On the way, a mistaken idea had to be overcome which might have been almost fatal to the young science. Influenced by Charcot's view of the traumatic origin of hysteria, one was readily inclined to accept as true and aetiologically significant the statements made by patients in which they ascribed their symptoms to passive sexual experiences in the first years of childhood—to put it bluntly, to seduction. When this aetiology broke down under the weight of its own improbability and contradiction in definitely ascertainable circumstances, the result at first was helpless bewilderment. Analysis had led back to these infantile sexual traumas by the right path, and yet they were not true. The firm ground of reality was gone. At that time I would gladly have given up the whole work, just as my esteemed predecessor, Breuer, had done when he made his unwelcome discovery. Perhaps I persevered only because I no longer had any choice and could not then begin again at anything else. At last came the reflection that, after all, one had no right to despair because one has been deceived in one's expectations; one must revise those expectations. If hysterical subjects trace back their symptoms to traumas that are fictitious, then the new fact which emerges is precisely that they create such scenes in *phantasy*, and this psychical reality requires to be taken into account alongside practical reality. This reflection was soon followed by the discovery that these phantasies were intended to cover up the auto-erotic activity of the first years of childhood, to embellish it and raise it to a higher plane. And now, from behind the phantasies, the whole range of a child's sexual life came to light.[1]

With this sexual activity of the first years of childhood the inherited constitution of the individual also came into its own. Disposition and experience are here linked up in an indissoluble aetiological unity. For *disposition* exaggerates impressions which would otherwise have been completely commonplace and have had no effect, so that they become traumas giving rise to stimulations and fixations; while *experiences* awaken factors in the disposition which, without them, might have long remained dormant and perhaps never have developed. The last word on the subject of traumatic aetiology was spoken later by Abraham [1907], when he pointed out that the sexual constitution which is peculiar to children is precisely calculated to provoke sexual experiences of a particular kind—namely traumas.

In the beginning, my statements about infantile sexuality were founded almost exclusively on the findings of analysis in adults which led back into the past. I had no opportunity of direct observations on children. It was therefore a very great triumph when it became possible years later to confirm almost all my inferences by direct observation and the analysis of very young children—a triumph that lost some of its magnitude as one gradually realized that the nature of the discovery was such that one should really be ashamed of having had to make it. The further one carried these observations on children, the more self-evident the facts became; but the more astonishing, too, did it become that one had taken so much trouble to overlook them.

Such a certain conviction of the existence and importance of infantile sexuality can, however, only be obtained by the method of analysis, by pursuing the symptoms and peculiarities of neurotics back to their ultimate sources, the discovery of

---

[1] [Freud's contemporary account of this rectification of his theory will be found in his letter to Fliess of September 21, 1897 (1950*a*, Letter 69). His first explicit published acknowledgement of it was made almost ten years later in a paper on sexuality in the neuroses (1906*a*). He further revised his views in Lecture XXXIII of the *New Introductory Lectures* (1933*a*), (Norton, 1965).]

which then explains whatever is explicable in them and enables whatever is modifiable to be changed. I can understand that one would arrive at different results if, as C. G. Jung has recently done, one first forms a theoretical conception of the nature of the sexual instinct and then seeks to explain the life of children on that basis. A conception of this kind is bound to be selected arbitrarily or in accordance with irrelevant considerations, and runs the risk of proving inadequate for the field to which one is seeking to apply it. It is true that the analytic method, too, leads to certain ultimate difficulties and obscurities in regard to sexuality and its relation to the total life of the individual. But these problems cannot be got rid of by speculation; they must await solution through other observations or through observations in other fields.

I need say little about the interpretation of dreams. It came as the first-fruits of the technical innovation I had adopted when, following a dim presentiment, I decided to replace hypnosis by free association. My desire for knowledge had not at the start been directed towards understanding dreams. I do not know of any outside influence which drew my interest to them or inspired me with any helpful expectations. Before Breuer and I ceased to meet I only just had time to tell him in a single sentence that I now understood how to translate dreams. Since this was how the discovery came about, it followed that the *symbolism* in the language of dreams was almost the last thing to become accessible to me, for the dreamer's associations help very little towards understanding symbols. I have held fast to the habit of always studying things themselves before looking for information about them in books, and therefore I was able to establish the symbolism of dreams for myself before I was led to it by Scherner's work on the subject [1861]. It was only later that I came to appreciate to its full extent this mode of expression of dreams. This was partly through the influence of the works of Stekel, who at first did such very creditable work but afterwards went totally astray.[1] The close connection between psycho-analytic dream-interpretation and the art of interpreting dreams as practised and held in such high esteem in

[1] [A longer discussion of Stekel's influence is contained in a passage added by Freud in 1925 to the section on symbolism, Chapter VI (E), in *The Interpretation of Dreams* (1900a).]

antiquity only became clear to me much later. Later on I found the essential characteristic and most important part of my dream theory—the derivation of dream-distortion from an internal conflict, a kind of inner dishonesty—in a writer who was ignorant, it is true, of medicine, though not of philosophy, the famous engineer J. Popper, who published his *Phantasien eines Realisten* [1899] under the name of Lynkeus.[1]

The interpretation of dreams became a solace and a support to me in those arduous first years of analysis, when I had to master the technique, clinical phenomena and therapy of the neuroses all at the same time. At that period I was completely isolated and in the network of problems and accumulation of difficulties I often dreaded losing my bearings and also my confidence. There were often patients with whom an unaccountably long time elapsed before my hypothesis, that a neurosis was bound to become intelligible through analysis, proved true; but these patients' dreams, which might be regarded as analogues of their symptoms, almost always confirmed the hypothesis.

It was only my success in this direction that enabled me to persevere. The result is that I have acquired a habit of gauging the measure of a psychologist's understanding by his attitude to dream-interpretation; and I have observed with satisfaction that most of the opponents of psycho-analysis avoid this field altogether or else display remarkable clumsiness if they attempt to deal with it. Moreover, I soon saw the necessity of carrying out a self-analysis, and this I did with the help of a series of my own dreams which led me back through all the events of my childhood; and I am still of the opinion to-day that this kind of analysis may suffice for anyone who is a good dreamer and not too abnormal.[2]

I think that by thus unrolling the story of the development of psycho-analysis I have shown what it is, better than by a

[1] [See Freud's two papers on this, 1923*f* and 1932*c*.—The word 'famous' in this sentence was added in 1924.]

[2] [Freud's contemporary account of important parts of his self-analysis will be found in the Fliess correspondence (1950*a*), particularly in Letters 70 and 71, written in October, 1897.—He did not always take such a favourable view of self-analysis as in the text above. For instance, in a letter to Fliess of November 14, 1897 (1950*a*, Letter 75), he wrote: 'My self-analysis is still interrupted and I have realized the

systematic description of it. I did not at first perceive the peculiar nature of what I had discovered. I unhesitatingly sacrificed my growing popularity as a doctor, and the increase in attendance during my consulting hours, by making a systematic enquiry into the sexual factors involved in the causation of my patients' neuroses; and this brought me a great many new facts which finally confirmed my conviction of the practical importance of the sexual factor. I innocently addressed a meeting of the Vienna Society for Psychiatry and Neurology with Krafft-Ebing [1] in the chair [cf. Freud, 1896c], expecting that the material losses I had willingly undergone would be made up for by the interest and recognition of my colleagues. I treated my discoveries as ordinary contributions to science and hoped they would be received in the same spirit. But the silence which my communications met with, the void which formed itself about me, the hints that were conveyed to me, gradually made me realize that assertions on the part played by sexuality in the aetiology of the neuroses cannot count upon meeting with the same kind of treatment as other communications. I understood that from now onwards I was one of those who have 'disturbed the sleep of the world', as Hebbel says,[2] and that I could not

reason. I can only analyse myself with the help of knowledge obtained objectively (like an outsider). Genuine self-analysis is impossible; otherwise there would be no [neurotic] illness. Since I still find some puzzles in my patients, they are bound to hold me up in my self-analysis.' Similarly, near the end of his life, in a short note on a parapraxis (1935b), he remarked in passing: 'In self-analysis the danger of incompleteness is particularly great. One is too soon satisfied with a part explanation, behind which resistance may easily be keeping back something that is more important perhaps.' Against these may be set the cautiously appreciative words which he prefaced to a paper by E. Pickworth Farrow (1926) giving the findings of a self-analysis (Freud, 1926c). In the case of *training* analyses at all events, he speaks strongly in favour of the need for analysis by some other person—for instance, in one of his papers on technique written not long before the present paper (1912e) and again in the very much later 'Analysis Terminable and Interminable' (1937c).]

[1] [R. von Krafft-Ebing (1840–1903) was Professor of Psychiatry at Strasbourg 1872–3, at Graz 1873–89, where he also directed the provincial mental hospital, and at Vienna 1889–1902. He was also distinguished for his work on criminology, neurology and psychopathia sexualis.]

[2] [A reference to Kandaules' words to Gyges in Hebbel's *Gyges und sein Ring*, Act V, Scene 1.]

reckon upon objectivity and tolerance. Since, however, my conviction of the general accuracy of my observations and conclusions grew even stronger, and since neither my confidence in my own judgement nor my moral courage were precisely small, the outcome of the situation could not be in doubt. I made up my mind to believe that it had been my fortune to discover some particularly important facts and connections, and I was prepared to accept the fate that sometimes accompanies such discoveries.

I pictured the future as follows:—I should probably succeed in maintaining myself by means of the therapeutic success of the new procedure, but science would ignore me entirely during my lifetime; some decades later, someone else would infallibly come upon the same things—for which the time was not now ripe—would achieve recognition for them and bring me honour as a forerunner whose failure had been inevitable. Meanwhile, like Robinson Crusoe, I settled down as comfortably as possible on my desert island. When I look back to those lonely years, away from the pressures and confusions of to-day, it seems like a glorious heroic age. My 'splendid isolation' [1] was not without its advantages and charms. I did not have to read any publications, nor listen to any ill-informed opponents; I was not subject to influence from any quarter; there was nothing to hustle me. I learnt to restrain speculative tendencies and to follow the unforgotten advice of my master, Charcot: to look at the same things again and again until they themselves begin to speak. [2] My publications, which I was able to place with a little trouble, could always lag far behind my knowledge, and could be postponed as long as I pleased, since there was no doubtful 'priority' to be defended. *The Interpretation of Dreams*, for instance, was finished in all essentials at the beginning of 1896 [3] but was not written out until the summer of 1899. The analysis of 'Dora' was over at the end of 1899 [1900];[4] the case history was written in the next two weeks, but was not published until 1905. Meanwhile my writings were not reviewed in the medical journals, or, if as an exception they *were* reviewed, they were dismissed with

[1] [In English in the original.]
[2] [The sentence appears, in slightly different words, in Freud's obituary of Charcot (1893*f*).]
[3] [This statement perhaps calls for some qualification.]
[4] [See footnote 2, p. 10].

expressions of scornful or pitying superiority. Occasionally a colleague would make some reference to me in one of his publications; it would be very short and not at all flattering—words such as 'eccentric', 'extreme', or 'very peculiar' would be used. It once happened that an assistant at the clinic in Vienna where I gave my University lectures asked me for permission to attend the course. He listened very attentively and said nothing; after the last lecture was over he offered to join me outside. As we walked away, he told me that with his chief's knowledge he had written a book combating my views; he regretted very much, however, that he had not first learnt more about them from my lectures, for in that case he would have written much of it differently. He had indeed enquired at the clinic whether he had not better first read *The Interpretation of Dreams*, but had been advised against doing so—it was not worth the trouble. He then himself compared the structure of my theory, so far as he now understood it, with that of the Catholic Church as regards its internal solidity. In the interests of the salvation of his soul, I shall assume that this remark implied a certain amount of appreciation. But he concluded by saying that it was too late to alter anything in his book, since it was already in print. Nor did my colleague think it necessary later to make any public avowal of his change of views on the subject of psycho-analysis; but preferred, in his capacity as a regular reviewer for a medical journal, to follow its development with flippant comments.[1]

Whatever personal sensitiveness I possessed became blunted during those years, to my advantage. I was saved from becoming embittered, however, by a circumstance which is not always present to help lonely discoverers. Such people are as a rule tormented by the need to account for the lack of sympathy or the aversion of their contemporaries, and feel this attitude as a distressing contradiction of the security of their own sense of conviction. There was no need for me to feel so; for psycho-analytic theory enabled me to understand this attitude in my contemporaries and to see it as a necessary consequence of fundamental analytic premisses. If it was true that the set of facts I had discovered were kept from the knowledge of patients themselves by internal resistances of an affective kind, then these resistances would be bound to appear in healthy people too, as

[1] [A sequel to this anecdote will be found at the beginning of Section V of Freud's *Autobiographical Study* (1925*d*), (Norton, 1963).]

soon as some external source confronted them with what was repressed. It was not surprising that they should be able to justify this rejection of my ideas on intellectual grounds though it was actually affective in origin. The same thing happened equally often with patients; the arguments they advanced were the same and were not precisely brilliant. In Falstaff's words, reasons are 'as plenty as blackberries'.[1] The only difference was that with patients one was in a position to bring pressure to bear on them so as to induce them to get insight into their resistances and overcome them, whereas one had to do without this advantage in dealing with people who were ostensibly healthy. How to compel these healthy people to examine the matter in a cool and scientifically objective spirit was an unsolved problem which was best left to time to clear up. In the history of science one can clearly see that often the very proposition which has at first called out nothing but contradiction has later come to be accepted, although no new proofs in support of it have been brought forward.

It was hardly to be expected, however, that during the years when I alone represented psycho-analysis I should develop any particular respect for the world's opinion or any bias towards intellectual appeasement.

[1] [*I Henry IV*, ii, 4.]

II

From the year 1902 onwards, a number of young doctors gathered round me with the express intention of learning, practising and spreading the knowledge of psycho-analysis. The stimulus came from a colleague who had himself experienced the beneficial effects of analytic therapy.[1] Regular meetings took place on certain evenings at my house, discussions were held according to certain rules and the participants endeavoured to find their bearings in this new and strange field of research and to interest others in it. One day a young man who had passed through a technical training college introduced himself with a manuscript which showed very unusual comprehension. We persuaded him to go through the *Gymnasium* [Secondary School] and the University and to devote himself to the non-medical side of psycho-analysis. The little society acquired in him a zealous and dependable secretary and I gained in Otto Rank a most loyal helper and co-worker.[2]

The small circle soon expanded, and in the course of the next few years often changed its composition. On the whole I could tell myself that it was hardly inferior, in wealth and variety of talent, to the staff of any clinical teacher one could think of. It included from the beginning the men who were later to play such a considerable, if not always a welcome, part in the history of the psycho-analytic movement. At that time, however, one could not yet guess at these developments. I had every reason to be satisfied, and I think I did everything possible to impart my own knowledge and experience to the others. There were only two inauspicious circumstances which at last estranged me inwardly from the group. I could not succeed in establishing among its members the friendly relations that ought to obtain between men who are all engaged upon the same difficult work; nor was I able to stifle the disputes about priority for which there were so many opportunities under these conditions of work in common. The difficulties in the way of giving

[1] [Wilhelm Stekel.]

[2] [*Footnote added* 1924:] Now director of the Internationaler Psycho-analytischer Verlag [International Psycho-Analytical Publishing House] and editor of the *Zeitschrift* and *Imago* from their inception [see below, p. 47].

instruction in the practice of psycho-analysis, which are quite particularly great and are responsible for much in the present dissensions, were evident already in this private Vienna Psycho-Analytical Society. I myself did not venture to put forward a still unfinished technique and a theory still in the making with an authority which would probably have enabled the others to avoid some wrong turnings and ultimate disasters. The self-reliance of intellectual workers, their early independence of their teacher, is always gratifying from a psychological point of view; but it is only of advantage to science if those workers fulfil certain personal conditions which are none too common. For psycho-analysis in particular a long and severe discipline and training in self-discipline would have been required. In view of the courage displayed by their devotion to a subject so much frowned upon and so poor in prospects, I was disposed to tolerate much among the members to which I should otherwise have made objection. Besides doctors, the circle included others —men of education who had recognized something important in psycho-analysis: writers, painters and so on. My *Interpretation of Dreams* and my book on jokes, among others, had shown from the beginning that the theories of psycho-analysis cannot be restricted to the medical field, but are capable of application to a variety of other mental sciences.

In 1907 the situation changed all at once and contrary to all expectations. It appeared that psycho-analysis had unobtrusively awakened interest and gained friends, and that there were even some scientific workers who were ready to acknowledge it. A communication from Bleuler[1] had informed me before this that my works had been studied and made use of in the Burghölzli. In January 1907, the first member of the Zurich clinic came to Vienna—Dr. Eitingon.[2] Other visits followed, which led to an animated exchange of ideas. Finally, on the invitation of C. G. Jung, at that time still assistant physician at the Burghölzli, a first meeting took place at Salzburg in the spring of 1908, which brought together friends of psycho-analysis from Vienna, Zurich and other places. One of the

[1] [Eugen Bleuler (1857–1939), the well-known psychiatrist, then head of the Burghölzli, the public mental hospital at Zurich.]

[2] [*Footnote added* 1924:] The subsequent founder of the 'Psycho-Analytic Policlinic' in Berlin. [See two short notes on this by Freud (1923*g* and 1930*b*).]

results of this first Psycho-Analytical Congress was the founding of a periodical called the *Jahrbuch für psychoanalytische und psychopathologische Forschungen* [see below, p. 46], under the direction of Bleuler and Freud and edited by Jung, which first appeared in 1909. This publication gave expression to an intimate co-operation between Vienna and Zurich.

I have repeatedly acknowledged with gratitude the great services rendered by the Zurich School of Psychiatry in the spread of psycho-analysis, particularly by Bleuler and Jung, and I have no hesitation in doing so again, even in the greatly altered circumstances of the present. True, it was not the support of the Zurich School which first directed the attention of the scientific world to psycho-analysis at that time. What had happened was that the latency period had expired and everywhere psycho-analysis was becoming the object of ever-increasing interest. But in all other places this accession of interest at first produced nothing but a very emphatic repudiation, mostly a quite passionate one; whereas in Zurich, on the contrary, agreement on general lines was the dominant note. Moreover, nowhere else did such a compact little group of adherents exist, or could a public clinic be placed at the service of psycho-analytic researches, or was there a clinical teacher who included psycho-analytic theories as an integral part of his psychiatric course. The Zurich group thus became the nucleus of the small band who were fighting for the recognition of analysis. The only opportunity of learning the new art and working at it in practice lay there. Most of my followers and co-workers at the present time came to me by way of Zurich, even those who were geographically much nearer to Vienna than to Switzerland. In relation to Western Europe, which contains the great centres of our culture, the position of Vienna is an outlying one; and its prestige has for many years been affected by strong prejudices. Representatives of all the most important nations congregate in Switzerland, where intellectual activity is so lively; a focus of infection there was bound to be of great importance for the spread of the 'psychical epidemic', as Hoche of Freiburg has called it.[1]

---

[1] [Alfred Hoche (b. 1865), Professor of Psychiatry at Freiburg, was particularly vehement and abusive in his attacks on psycho-analysis. He read a paper on it at a medical congress at Baden-Baden with the title 'A Psychical Epidemic among Doctors'. (Hoche, 1910.)]

According to the evidence of a colleague who witnessed developments at the Burghölzli, it appears that psycho-analysis awakened interest there very early. In Jung's work on occult phenomena, published in 1902, there was already an allusion to my book on dream-interpretation. From 1903 or 1904, says my informant, psycho-analysis was in the forefront of interest. After personal relations between Vienna and Zurich had been established, an informal society was also started, in the middle of 1907, in the Burghölzli, where the problems of psycho-analysis were discussed at regular meetings. In the alliance between the Vienna and Zurich schools the Swiss were by no means mere recipients. They had already produced very creditable scientific work, the results of which were of service to psycho-analysis. The association experiments started by the Wundt School had been interpreted by them in a psycho-analytic sense, and had proved applicable in unexpected ways. By this means it had become possible to arrive at rapid experimental confirmation of psycho-analytic observations and to demonstrate directly to students certain connections which an analyst would only have been able to tell them about. The first bridge linking up experimental psychology with psycho-analysis had been built.

In psycho-analytic treatment, association experiments enable a provisional, qualitative analysis of the case to be made, but they furnish no essential contribution to the technique and can be dispensed with in carrying out analyses. More important, however, was another achievement by the Zurich school, or its leaders, Bleuler and Jung. The former showed that light could be thrown on a large number of purely psychiatric cases by adducing the same processes as have been recognized through psycho-analysis to obtain in dreams and neuroses (Freudian mechanisms); and Jung [1907] successfully applied the analytic method of interpretation to the most alien and obscure phenomena of dementia praecox [schizophrenia], so that their sources in the life-history and interests of the patient came clearly to light. After this it was impossible for psychiatrists to ignore psycho-analysis any longer. Bleuler's great work on schizophrenia (1911), in which the psycho-analytic point of view was placed on an equal footing with the clinical systematic one, completed this success.

I will not omit to point out a divergence which was already

at that time noticeable in the direction taken by the work of the two schools. As early as in 1897 [1] I had published the analysis of a case of schizophrenia, which however was of a paranoid character, so that the solution of it could not take away from the impression made by Jung's analyses. But to me the important point had been, not so much the possibility of interpreting the symptoms, as the psychical mechanism of the disease, and above all the agreement of this mechanism with that of hysteria, which had already been discovered. At that time no light had yet been thrown on the differences between the two mechanisms. For I was then already aiming at a libido theory of the neuroses, which was to explain all neurotic and psychotic phenomena as proceeding from abnormal vicissitudes of the libido, that is, as diversions from its normal employment. This point of view was missed by the Swiss investigators. As far as I know, even to-day Bleuler maintains the view that the various forms of dementia praecox have an organic causation; and at the Salzburg Congress in 1908 Jung, whose book on this disease had appeared in 1907, supported the toxic theory of its causation, which takes no account of the libido theory, although it is true that it does not rule it out. Later on (1912) he came to grief on this same point, by making too much of the material which he had previously refused to employ.

There is a third contribution made by the Swiss School, probably to be ascribed entirely to Jung, which I do not value so highly as others do whose concern with these matters is more remote. I refer to the theory of 'complexes' which grew out of the *Diagnostische Assoziationsstudien* [*Studies in Word-Association*] (1906). It has neither itself produced a psychological theory, nor has it proved capable of easy incorporation into the context of psycho-analytic theory. The word 'complex', on the other hand, has become naturalized, so to speak, in psycho-analytic language; it is a convenient and often indispensable term for summing up a psychological state descriptively. [2] None of the other

[1] [This wrong date appears in all the German editions. The case was published in May, 1896. It occupies Section III of Freud's second paper on 'The Neuro-Psychoses of Defence' (1896*b*).]

[2] [Freud seems to have first borrowed the term from Jung in a paper on evidence in legal proceedings (1906*c*). He himself, however, had used the word in what seems a very similar sense long before, in a footnote to the case of Frau Emmy von N. in *Studies on Hysteria* (1895*d*).]

terms coined by psycho-analysis for its own needs has achieved such widespread popularity or been so misapplied to the detriment of the construction of clearer concepts. Analysts began to speak among themselves of a 'return of a complex' where they meant a 'return of the repressed', or fell into the habit of saying 'I have a complex against him', where the only correct expression would have been 'a resistance against him'.

In the years following 1907, when the schools of Vienna and Zurich were united, psycho-analysis made the extraordinary surge forward of which the momentum is felt even to-day; this is shown both by the spread of psycho-analytic literature and by the constant increase in the number of doctors who are practising or studying it, as well as by the frequency of the attacks made on it at Congresses and in learned societies. It has penetrated into the most distant lands and has everywhere not merely startled psychiatrists but commanded the attention of the educated public and of scientific workers in other fields. Havelock Ellis, who has followed its development with sympathy though without ever calling himself an adherent, wrote in 1911 in a report for the Australasian Medical Congress: 'Freud's psycho-analysis is now championed and carried out not only in Austria and in Switzerland, but in the United States, in England, in India, in Canada, and, I doubt not, in Australasia.' [1] A physician from Chile (probably a German) spoke at the International Congress at Buenos Aires in 1910 in support of the existence of infantile sexuality and commended highly the effects of psycho-analytic therapy on obsessional symptoms. [2] An English neurologist in Central India (Berkeley-Hill[3]) informed me, through a distinguished colleague who was visiting Europe, that the analyses of Mohammedan Indians which he had carried out showed that the aetiology of their neuroses was no different from what we find in our European patients.

The introduction of psycho-analysis into North America was accompanied by very special marks of honour. In the autumn

[1] Havelock Ellis, 1911. [Freud himself contributed a paper to the same Congress in Sydney (1913*m* [1911]).]

[2] G. Greve, 1910. [Freud wrote an abstract of this (1911*g*).]

[3] [The name was added in 1924.]

of 1909, Stanley Hall, the President of Clark University, Worcester, Massachusetts, invited Jung and myself to take part in the celebration of the twentieth anniversary of the foundation of the University by giving a number of lectures in German. To our great surprise, we found the members of that small but highly esteemed University for the study of education and philosophy so unprejudiced that they were acquainted with all the literature of psycho-analysis and had given it a place in their lectures to students. In prudish America it was possible, in academic circles at least, to discuss freely and scientifically everything that in ordinary life is regarded as objectionable. The five lectures which I improvised in Worcester appeared in an English translation in the *American Journal of Psychology* [1910*a*], and were shortly afterwards published in German under the title *Über Psychoanalyse*. Jung read a paper on diagnostic association experiments and another on conflicts in the mind of the child.[1] We were rewarded with the honorary degree of Doctor of Laws. During that week of celebrations at Worcester, psycho-analysis was represented by five men: besides Jung and myself, there were Ferenczi, who had joined me for the journey, Ernest Jones, then at the University of Toronto (Canada) and now in London, and A. A. Brill, who was already practising psycho-analysis in New York.

The most important personal relationship which arose from the meeting at Worcester was that with James J. Putnam, Professor of Neuropathology at Harvard University. Some years before, he had expressed an unfavourable opinion of psychoanalysis, but now he rapidly became reconciled to it and recommended it to his countrymen and his colleagues in a series of lectures which were as rich in content as they were brilliant in form. The esteem he enjoyed throughout America on account of his high moral character and unflinching love of truth was of great service to psycho-analysis and protected it against the denunciations which in all probability would otherwise quickly have overwhelmed it. Later on, yielding too much to the strong ethical and philosophical bent of his nature, Putnam made what seems to me an impossible demand—he expected psychoanalysis to place itself at the service of a particular moral-philosophical conception of the Universe—but he remains the

[1] [Jung 1910*a* and 1910*b*.]

chief pillar of the psycho-analytic movement in his native land.[1]

For the further spread of this movement Brill and Jones deserve the greatest credit: in their writings they drew their countrymen's attention with unremitting assiduity to the easily observable fundamental facts of everyday life, of dreams and neurosis. Brill has contributed still further to this effect by his medical practice and by his translations of my works, and Jones by his instructive lectures and by his skill in debate at congresses in America.[2] The absence of any deep-rooted scientific tradition in America and the much less stringent rule of official authority there have been of decided advantage to the impetus given by Stanley Hall. It was characteristic of that country that from the beginning professors and superintendents of mental hospitals showed as much interest in analysis as independent practitioners. But it is clear that precisely for this reason the ancient centres of culture, where the greatest resistance has been displayed, must be the scene of the decisive struggle over psycho-analysis.

Among European countries France has hitherto shown itself the least disposed to welcome psycho-analysis, although useful work in French by A. Maeder of Zurich has provided easy access to its theories. The first indications of sympathy came from the provinces: Morichau-Beauchant (Poitiers) was the first Frenchman to adhere publicly to psycho-analysis. Régis[3] and Hesnard (Bordeaux) have recently [1914] attempted to disperse the prejudices of their countrymen against the new ideas by an exhaustive presentation, which, however, is not always understanding and takes special exception to symbolism.[4] In Paris itself, a conviction still seems to reign (to which Janet himself gave eloquent expression at the Congress[5] in London in 1913) that everything good in psycho-analysis is a repetition of Janet's views with insignificant modifications, and that every-

[1] [Footnote added 1924:] See Putnam's Addresses on Psycho-Analysis, 1921. [Freud contributed a preface to this (1921a).]—Putnam died in 1918. [See Freud's obituary of him (1919b).]

[2] The publications of both authors have appeared in collected volumes: Brill, 1912, and Ernest Jones, 1913.

[3] [E. Régis (1855–1918) was Professor of Psychiatry at Bordeaux from 1905.]

[4] [Before 1924 this read 'an exhaustive and understanding presentation which only took exception to symbolism'.]

[5] [The International Medical Congress.]

thing else in it is bad. At this Congress itself, indeed, Janet had to submit to a number of corrections by Ernest Jones, who was able to point out to him his insufficient knowledge of the subject.[1] Even though we deny his claims, however, we cannot forget the value of his work on the psychology of the neuroses.

In Italy, after several promising starts, no real interest was forthcoming. To Holland analysis found early access through personal connections: Van Emden, Van Ophuijsen, Van Renterghem (*Freud en zijn School* [1913]) and the two Stärckes are actively occupied with it both in practice and theory.[2] In scientific circles in England interest in analysis has developed very slowly, but there is reason to expect that the sense for the practical and the passionate love of justice in the English will ensure it a brilliant future there.

In Sweden, P. Bjerre, who succeeded to Wetterstrand's practice, gave up hypnotic suggestion, at least for the time, in favour of analytic treatment. R. Vogt (Christiania) had already shown an appreciation of psycho-analysis in his *Psykiatriens grundtraek*, published in 1907; so that the first text-book of psychiatry to refer to psycho-analysis was written in Norwegian. In Russia, psycho-analysis has become generally known and has spread widely; almost all my writings, as well as those of other adherents of analysis, have been translated into Russian. But a really penetrating comprehension of analytic theories has not yet been evinced in Russia; so that the contributions of Russian physicians are at present not very notable. The only trained analyst there is M. Wulff who practises in Odessa. It is principally due to L. Jekels that psycho-analysis has been introduced to Polish scientific and literary circles. Hungary, so near geographically to Austria, and so far from it scientifically, has produced only one collaborator, S. Ferenczi, but one that indeed outweighs a whole society.[3]

---

[1] [Cf. Janet (1913) and Jones (1915).]

[2] The first *official* recognition of dream-interpretation and psychoanalysis in Europe was extended to them by the psychiatrist Jelgersma, Rector of the University of Leyden, in his rectorial address on February 9, 1914.

[3] (*Footnote added* 1923:) It is not my intention, of course, to bring this account, written in 1914, 'up to date' [in English in the original]. I will only add a few remarks to indicate how the picture has altered in the interval, which includes the World War. In Germany a gradual infiltration

As regards the position of psycho-analysis in Germany, it can only be said that it forms the centre-point of scientific discussions and provokes the most emphatic expressions of disagreement both among doctors and laymen; these are not yet at an end, but are constantly flaring up again,) sometimes with greater intensity. No official educational bodies there have up to now recognized psycho-analysis. Successful practitioners who employ it are few; only a few institutions, such as Binswanger's in Kreuzlingen (on Swiss soil) and Marcinowski's in Holstein, have opened their doors to it. One of the most prominent representatives of analysis, Karl Abraham, at one time an assistant of Bleuler's, maintains himself in the critical atmosphere of Berlin. One might wonder that this state of things should have continued unaltered for several years if one did not know that the account I have given only represents external appearances. Too much significance should not be attributed to rejection by the official representatives of science and heads of institutions, and by the followers dependent on them. It is natural that its opponents should give loud expression to their views, while its intimidated adherents keep silence. Some of the latter, whose first contributions to analysis raised favourable expectations, have later withdrawn from the movement under the pressure of circumstances. The movement itself advances

of analytic theories into clinical psychiatry is taking place, though this is not always admitted. The French translations of my works that have been appearing during the last few years have finally aroused a keen interest in psycho-analysis even in France, though for the moment this is more active in literary circles than in scientific ones. In Italy M. Levi Bianchini (of Nocera Superiore) and Edoardo Weiss (of Trieste) have come forward as translators and champions of psycho-analysis (cf. the *Biblioteca Psicoanalitica Italiana*). A collected edition of my works which is appearing in Madrid (translated by Lopez Ballesteros) is evidence of the lively interest taken in it in Spanish-speaking countries (Prof. H. Delgado in Lima). As regards England, the prophecy which I have made above seems to be in steady course of fulfilment; a special centre for the study of analysis has been formed at Calcutta in British India. In North America it is still true that the depth of understanding of analysis does not keep pace with its popularity. In Russia, since the Revolution, psycho-analytic work has begun afresh at several centres. In Poland the *Polska Bibljoteka Psychoanalityczna* is now appearing. In Hungary a brilliant analytic school is flourishing under the leadership of Ferenczi. (Cf. the Festschrift issued in honour of his fiftieth birthday [which included an appreciation by Freud, 1923*i*].) At the present time the Scandinavian countries are still the least receptive.

surely though silently; it is constantly gaining new adherents among psychiatrists and laymen, it brings in a growing stream of new readers for psycho-analytic literature and for that very reason drives its opponents to ever more violent defensive efforts. At least a dozen times in recent years, in reports of the proceedings of certain congresses and scientific bodies or in reviews of certain publications, I have read that now psycho-analysis is dead, defeated and disposed of once and for all. The best answer to all this would be in the terms of Mark Twain's telegram to the newspaper which had falsely published news of his death: 'Report of my death greatly exaggerated.' After each of these obituaries psycho-analysis regularly gained new adherents and co-workers or acquired new channels of publicity. After all, being declared dead was an advance on being buried in silence.

Hand in hand with this expansion of psycho-analysis in space went an expansion in content; it extended from the field of the neuroses and psychiatry to other fields of knowledge. I shall not treat this aspect of the development of our discipline in much detail, since this has been done with great success by Rank and Sachs [1913] in a volume (one of Löwenfeld's *Grenzfragen*) which deals exhaustively with precisely this side of analytic research. Moreover, this development is still in its infancy; it has been little worked at, consists mostly of tentative beginnings and in part of no more than plans. No reasonable person will see any grounds for reproach in this. An enormous mass of work confronts a small number of workers, most of whom have their main occupation elsewhere and can bring only the qualifications of an amateur to bear on the technical problems of these unfamiliar fields of science. These workers, who derive from psycho-analysis, make no secret of their amateurishness. Their aim is merely to act as sign-posts and stop-gaps for the specialists, and to put the analytic technique and principles at their disposal against a time when they in turn shall take up the work. That the results achieved are nevertheless not inconsiderable is due partly to the fruitfulness of the analytic method, and partly to the circumstance that there are already a few investigators who are not doctors, and have taken up the application of psycho-analysis to the mental sciences as their profession in life.

Most of these applications of analysis naturally go back to a hint in my earliest analytic writings. The analytic examination of neurotic people and the neurotic symptoms of normal people necessitated the assumption of psychological conditions which could not possibly be limited to the field in which they had been discovered. In this way analysis not only provided us with the explanation of pathological phenomena, but revealed their connection with normal mental life and disclosed unsuspected relationships between psychiatry and the most various other sciences dealing with activities of the mind. Certain typical dreams, for instance, yielded an explanation of some myths and fairy-tales. Riklin [1908] and Abraham [1909] followed this hint and initiated the researches into myths which have found their completion, in a manner complying with even expert standards, in Rank's works on mythology [e.g. 1909, 1911b]. Further investigation into dream-symbolism led to the heart of the problems of mythology, folklore (Jones [e.g. 1910 and 1912] and Storfer [1914]) and the abstractions of religion. A deep impression was made on all hearers at one of the psycho-analytical Congresses when a follower of Jung's demonstrated the correspondence between schizophrenic phantasies and the cosmogonies of primitive times and races.[1] Mythological material later received further elaboration (which, though open to criticism, was none the less very interesting) at the hands of Jung, in works attempting to correlate the neuroses with religious and mythological phantasies.

Another path led from the investigation of dreams to the analysis of works of imagination and ultimately to the analysis of their creators—writers and artists themselves. At an early stage it was discovered that dreams invented by writers will often yield to analysis in the same way as genuine ones. (Cf. 'Gradiva' [1907a].) The conception of unconscious mental activity made it possible to form a preliminary idea of the nature of imaginative creative writing; and the realization, gained in the study of neurotics, of the part played by the instinctual impulses enabled us to perceive the sources of artistic production and confronted us with two problems: how the artist reacts to this instigation and what means he employs to disguise his reactions.[2] Most analysts with general interests

---

[1] [Jan Nelken at the Weimar Congress in 1911. An expanded version of the paper will be found in Nelken, 1912.]

[2] Cf. Rank's *Der Künstler* [*The Artist*, 1907], analyses of imaginative writers by Sadger [1909], Reik [1912, etc.], and others, my own small

have contributed something to the solution of these problems, which are the most fascinating among the applications of psycho-analysis. Naturally, opposition was not lacking in this direction either on the part of people who knew nothing of analysis; it took the same form as it did in the original field of psycho-analytic research—the same misconceptions and vehement rejections. It was only to be expected from the beginning that, whatever the regions into which psycho-analysis might penetrate, it would inevitably experience the same struggles with those already in possession of the field. These attempted invasions, however, have not yet stirred up the attention in some quarters which awaits them in the future. Among the strictly scientific applications of analysis to literature, Rank's exhaustive work on the theme of incest [1912] easily takes the first place. Its subject is bound to arouse the greatest unpopularity. Up to the present, little work based on psycho-analysis has been done in the sciences of language and history. I myself ventured the first approach to the problems of the psychology of religion by drawing a parallel between religious ritual and the ceremonials of neurotics (1907b).[1] Dr. Pfister, a pastor in Zurich, has traced back the origin of religious fanaticism to perverse eroticism in his book on the piety of Count von Zinzendorf [1910], as well as in other contributions. In the latest works of the Zurich school, however, we find analysis permeated with religious ideas rather than the opposite outcome that had been in view.

In the four essays with the title *Totem and Taboo* [1912–13] I have made an attempt to deal with the problems of social anthropology in the light of analysis; this line of investigation leads direct to the origins of the most important institutions of our civilization, of the structure of the state, of morality and religion, and, moreover, of the prohibition against incest and of conscience. It is no doubt too early to decide how far the conclusions thus reached will be able to withstand criticism.

The first example of an application of the analytic mode of thought to the problems of aesthetics was contained in my book on jokes [1905c]. Everything beyond this is still awaiting workers, who may expect a particularly rich harvest in this

work on a childhood memory of Leonardo da Vinci's [1910c], and Abraham's analysis of Segantini [1911].

[1] [All the German editions give this date wrongly as 1910.]

field. We are entirely without the co-operation of specialists in all these branches of knowledge, and in order to attract them Hanns Sachs, in 1912, founded the periodical *Imago* which is edited by him and Rank. A beginning has been made by Hitschmann and von Winterstein in throwing psycho-analytic light on philosophical systems and personalities, and here there is much need both of extended and of deeper investigation.

The revolutionary discoveries of psycho-analysis in regard to the mental life of children—the part played in it by sexual impulses (von Hug-Hellmuth [1913]), and the fate of those components of sexuality which become unserviceable in the function of reproduction—were bound early to direct attention to education and to stimulate an attempt to bring analytic points of view into the foreground in that field of work. Recognition is due to Dr. Pfister for having, with sincere enthusiasm, initiated the application of psycho-analysis in this direction and brought it to the notice of ministers of religion and those concerned with education. (Cf. *The Psycho-Analytic Method*, 1913.[1]) He has succeeded in gaining the sympathy and participation of a number of Swiss teachers in this. Other members of his profession are said to share his views but to have preferred nevertheless to remain cautiously in the background. In their retreat from psycho-analysis, a section of Vienna analysts seem to have arrived at a kind of combination of medicine and education.[2]

With this incomplete outline I have attempted to give some idea of the still incalculable wealth of connections which have come to light between medical psycho-analysis and other fields of science. There is material here for a generation of investigators to work at, and I do not doubt that the work will be carried out as soon as the resistances against psycho-analysis are overcome on its original ground.[3]

To write the story of these resistances would, I think, be both fruitless and inopportune at the present time. The story is not very creditable to the scientific men of our day. But I must add at once that it has never occurred to me to pour contempt upon the opponents of psycho-analysis merely because they were

[1] [Freud wrote a preface to this (1913*b*).]
[2] Adler and Furtmüller, *Heilen und Bilden* [*Healing and Educating*], 1914.
[3] See my two articles in *Scientia* (1913*j*).

opponents—apart from the few unworthy individuals, the adventurers and profiteers, who are always to be found on both sides in time of war. I knew very well how to account for the behaviour of these opponents and, moreover, I had learnt that psycho-analysis brings out the worst in everyone. But I made up my mind not to answer my opponents and, so far as my influence went, to restrain others from polemics. Under the peculiar conditions of the controversy over psycho-analysis it seemed to me very doubtful whether either public or written discussion would avail anything; it was certain which way the majority at congresses and meetings would go, and my faith in the reasonableness and good behaviour of the gentlemen who opposed me was not at any time great. Experience shows that only very few people are capable of remaining polite, to say nothing of objective, in a scientific dispute, and the impression made on me by scientific squabbles has always been odious. Perhaps this attitude on my part has been misunderstood; perhaps I have been thought so good-natured or so easily intimidated that no further notice need be taken of me. This was a mistake; I can be as abusive and enraged as anyone; but I have not the art of expressing the underlying emotions in a form suitable for publication and I therefore prefer to abstain completely.

Perhaps in some respects it would have been better if I had given free rein to my own passions and to those of others round me. We have all heard of the interesting attempt to explain psycho-analysis as a product of the Vienna milieu. As recently as in 1913 Janet was not ashamed to use this argument, although he himself is no doubt proud of being a Parisian, and Paris can scarcely claim to be a city of stricter morals than Vienna.[1] The suggestion is that psycho-analysis, and in particular its assertion that the neuroses are traceable to disturbances in sexual life, could only have originated in a town like Vienna—in an atmosphere of sensuality and immorality foreign to other cities—and that it is simply a reflection, a projection into theory, as it were, of these peculiar Viennese conditions. Now I am certainly no local patriot; but this theory about psycho-analysis always seems to me quite exceptionally senseless —so senseless, in fact, that I have sometimes been inclined to suppose that the reproach of being a citizen of Vienna is only

[1] [The last clause of this sentence was added in 1924.]

a euphemistic substitute for another reproach which no one would care to put forward openly.[1] If the premisses on which the argument rests were the opposite of what they are, then it might be worth giving it a hearing. If there were a town in which the inhabitants imposed exceptional restrictions on themselves as regards sexual satisfaction, and if at the same time they exhibited a marked tendency to severe neurotic disorders, that town might certainly give rise in an observer's mind to the idea that the two circumstances had some connection with each other, and might suggest that one was contingent on the other. But neither of these assumptions is true of Vienna. The Viennese are no more abstinent and no more neurotic than the inhabitants of any other capital city. There is rather less embarrassment—less prudery—in regard to sexual relationships than in the cities of the West and North which are so proud of their chastity. These peculiar characteristics of Vienna would be more likely to mislead the observer on the causation of neurosis than to enlighten him on it.

Vienna has done everything possible, however, to deny her share in the origin of psycho-analysis. In no other place is the hostile indifference of the learned and educated section of the population so evident to the analyst as in Vienna.

It may be that my policy of avoiding wide publicity is to some extent responsible for this. If I had encouraged or allowed the medical societies of Vienna to occupy themselves with psycho-analysis in stormy debates which would have discharged all the passions and brought into the open all the reproaches and invectives that were on its opponents' tongues or in their hearts —then, perhaps, the ban on psycho-analysis would have been overcome by now and it would no longer be a stranger in its native city. As it is, the poet may be right when he makes his Wallenstein say:

> Doch das vergeben mir die Wiener nicht,
> dass ich um ein Spektakel sie betrog.[2]

The task to which I was not equal—that of demonstrating to the opponents of psycho-analysis *suaviter in modo* their injustice and arbitrariness—was undertaken and carried out most credit-

[1] [Presumably Freud's Jewish origin.]
[2] [Literally: 'But what the Viennese will not forgive me is having cheated them out of a spectacle.' Schiller, *Die Piccolomini*, II, 7.]

ably by Bleuler in a paper written in 1910, 'Freud's Psycho-Analysis: A Defence and Some Critical Remarks'. It would seem so natural for me to praise this work (which offers criticisms in both directions) that I will hasten to say what I take exception to in it. It seems to me still to display partiality, to be too lenient to the faults of the opponents of psycho-analysis and too severe on the shortcomings of its adherents. This trait in it may possibly explain why the opinion of a psychiatrist of such high repute, such undoubted ability and independence, failed to carry more weight with his colleagues. The author of *Affectivity* (1906) ought not to be surprised if the influence of a work is determined not by the strength of its arguments but by its affective tone. Another part of its influence—its influence on the followers of psycho-analysis—was destroyed later by Bleuler himself, when in 1913 he showed the reverse side of his attitude to psycho-analysis in his 'Criticism of the Freudian Theory'. In that paper he subtracts so much from the structure of psycho-analytic theory that our opponents may well be glad of the help given them by this champion of psycho-analysis. These adverse judgements of Bleuler's, however, are not based on new arguments or better observations. They rely simply on the state of his own knowledge, the inadequacy of which he no longer himself admits, as he did in his earlier works. It seemed therefore that an almost irreparable loss threatened psycho-analysis here. But in his last publication, 'Criticisms of my *Schizophrenia*' (1914), Bleuler rallies his forces in the face of the attacks made on him for having introduced psycho-analysis into his book on schizophrenia, and makes what he himself calls a 'presumptuous claim'. 'But now I will make a presumptuous claim: I consider that up to the present the various schools of psychology have contributed extremely little towards explaining the nature of psychogenic symptoms and diseases, but that depth-psychology offers something towards a psychology which still awaits creation and which physicians are in need of in order to understand their patients and to cure them rationally; and I even believe that in my *Schizophrenia* I have taken a very short step towards that understanding. The first two assertions are certainly correct; the last may be an error.'

Since by 'depth-psychology' he means nothing else but psycho-analysis, we may for the present be content with this acknowledgement.

III

Mach es kurz!
Am Jüngsten Tag ist's nur ein Furz! [1]

GOETHE

Two years after the first private Congress of psycho-analysts the second took place, this time at Nuremberg, in March, 1910. In the interval between them, influenced partly by the favourable reception in America, by the increasing hostility in German-speaking countries, and by the unforeseen acquisition of support from Zurich, I had conceived a project which with the help of my friend Ferenczi I carried out at this second Congress. What I had in mind was to organize the psychoanalytic movement, to transfer its centre to Zurich and to give it a chief who would look after its future career. As this scheme has met with much opposition among the adherents of psychoanalysis, I will set out my reasons for it in some detail. I hope that these will justify me, even though it turns out that what I did was in fact not very wise.

I judged that the new movement's association with Vienna was no recommendation but rather a handicap to it. A place in the heart of Europe like Zurich, where an academic teacher had opened the doors of his institution to psycho-analysis, seemed to me much more promising. I also took it that a second handicap lay in my own person, opinion about which was too much con-

---

[1] [Literally: 'Cut it short! On the Day of Judgement it is no more than a fart.' The lines occur in some ironic verses written late in Goethe's life (Grossherzog Wilhelm Ernst Ausgabe, **15,** 400–1). Satan is represented in them as bringing up a number of charges against Napoleon, and the words quoted by Freud are God the Father's reply. Freud had many years earlier (on December 4, 1896) quoted the same words in a letter to Fliess, as the suggested motto for a chapter on 'Resistance' (Freud, 1950a, Letter 51). Two possible explanations, not necessarily incompatible, may be offered for Freud's use of the quotation in the present connection. He may be applying the words to the criticisms put forward by the opponents of psycho-analysis, or he may be applying them ironically to himself for wasting his time on such trivialities.]

fused by the liking or hatred of the different sides: I was either compared to Columbus,[1] Darwin and Kepler, or abused as a general paralytic. I wished, therefore, to withdraw into the background both myself and the city where psycho-analysis first saw the light. Moreover, I was no longer young; I saw that there was a long road ahead, and I felt oppressed by the thought that the duty of being a leader should fall to me so late in life.[2] Yet I felt that there must be someone at the head. I knew only too well the pitfalls that lay in wait for anyone who became engaged in analysis, and hoped that many of them might be avoided if an authority could be set up who would be prepared to instruct and admonish. This position had at first been occupied by myself, owing to my fifteen years' start in experience which nothing could counterbalance. I felt the need of transferring this authority to a younger man, who would then as a matter of course take my place after my death. This man could only be C. G. Jung, since Bleuler was my contemporary in age; in favour of Jung were his exceptional talents, the contributions he had already made to psycho-analysis, his independent position and the impression of assured energy which his personality conveyed. In addition to this, he seemed ready to enter into a friendly relationship with me and for my sake to give up certain racial prejudices which he had previously permitted himself. I had no inkling at that time that in spite of all these advantages the choice was a most unfortunate one, that I had lighted upon a person who was incapable of tolerating the authority of another, but who was still less capable of wielding it himself, and whose energies were relentlessly devoted to the furtherance of his own interests.

I considered it necessary to form an official association because I feared the abuses to which psycho-analysis would be subjected as soon as it became popular. There should be some headquarters whose business it would be to declare: 'All this nonsense is nothing to do with analysis; this is not psycho-analysis.' At the sessions of the local groups (which together would constitute the international association) instruction should be given as to how psycho-analysis was to be conducted and doctors should be trained, whose activities would then receive a kind of guarantee. Moreover, it seemed to me desirable, since

[1] [This name was added in 1924.]
[2] [In 1910 Freud was 54.]

official science had pronounced its solemn ban upon psycho-analysis and had declared a boycott against doctors and institutions practising it, that the adherents of psycho-analysis should come together for friendly communication with one another and mutual support.

This and nothing else was what I hoped to achieve by founding the 'International Psycho-Analytical Association'. It was probably more than could be attained. Just as my opponents were to discover that it was not possible to stem the tide of the new movement, so I was to find that it would not proceed in the direction I wished to mark out for it. The proposals made by Ferenczi in Nuremberg were adopted, it is true; Jung was elected President and made Riklin his Secretary; the publication of a bulletin which should link the Central Executive with the local groups was resolved upon. The object of the Association was declared to be 'to foster and further the science of psycho-analysis founded by Freud, both as pure psychology and in its application to medicine and the mental sciences; and to promote mutual support among its members in all endeavours to acquire and to spread psycho-analytic knowledge'. The scheme was strongly opposed only by the Vienna group. Adler, in great excitement, expressed the fear that 'censorship and restrictions on scientific freedom' were intended. Finally the Viennese gave in, after having secured that the seat of the Association should be not Zurich, but the place of residence of the President for the time being, who was to be elected for two years.

At this Congress three local groups were constituted: one in Berlin, under the chairmanship of Abraham; one in Zurich, whose head had become the President of the whole Association; and one in Vienna, the direction of which I made over to Adler. A fourth group, in Budapest, could not be formed until later. Bleuler had not attended the Congress on account of illness, and later he evinced hesitation about joining the Association on general grounds; he let himself be persuaded to do so, it is true, after a personal conversation with me, but resigned again shortly afterwards as a result of disagreements in Zurich. This severed the connection between the Zurich local group and the Burghölzli institution.

One outcome of the Nuremberg Congress was the founding of the *Zentralblatt für Psychoanalyse* [*Central Journal for Psycho-Analysis*], for which purpose Adler and Stekel joined forces. It was obviously intended originally to represent the Opposition: it was meant to win back for Vienna the hegemony threatened by the election of Jung. But when the two founders of the journal, labouring under the difficulties of finding a publisher, assured me of their peaceful intentions and as a guarantee of their sincerity gave me a right of veto, I accepted the direction of it and worked energetically for the new organ; its first number appeared in September, 1910.

I will now continue the story of the Psycho-Analytical Congresses. The third Congress took place in September, 1911, at Weimar, and was even more successful than the previous ones in its general atmosphere and scientific interest. J. J. Putnam, who was present on this occasion, declared afterwards in America how much pleasure it had given him and expressed his respect for 'the mental attitude' of those who attended it, quoting some words I was said to have used in reference to them: 'They have learnt to tolerate a bit of truth.' (Putnam 1912.) It is a fact that no one who had attended scientific congresses could have failed to carry away a favourable impression of the Psycho-Analytical Association. I myself had conducted the first two Congresses and I had allowed every speaker time for his paper, leaving discussions to take place in private afterwards among the members. Jung, as President, took over the direction at Weimar and re-introduced formal discussions after each paper, which, however, did not give rise to any difficulties as yet.

A very different picture was presented by the fourth Congress, held in Munich two years later, in September, 1913. It is still fresh in the memory of all who were present. It was conducted by Jung in a disagreeable and incorrect manner; the speakers were restricted in time and the discussions overwhelmed the papers. By a malicious stroke of chance it happened that that evil genius, Hoche,[1] had settled in the very building in which the meetings were held. Hoche would have had no difficulty in convincing himself of the nonsense which the analysts made of his description of them as a fanatical sect blindly submissive to their leader. The fatiguing and unedifying proceedings ended in the re-election of Jung to the Presidency of the International Psycho-Analytical Association, which he accepted, although two-fifths of those present refused him their support. We dispersed without any desire to meet again.

[1] [See footnote, p. 27.]

At about the time of this Congress the strength of the International Psycho-Analytical Association was as follows. The local groups in Vienna, Berlin and Zurich had been formed at the Congress in Nuremberg as early as 1910. In May, 1911, a group at Munich under the chairmanship of Dr. L. Seif was added. In the same year the first American local group was formed under the chairmanship of A. A. Brill, with the name 'The New York Psychoanalytic Society'. At the Weimar Congress the foundation of a second American group was authorized; it came into existence during the following year under the name of 'The American Psychoanalytic Association', and included members from Canada and the whole of America; Putnam was elected President and Ernest Jones Secretary. Shortly before the Congress in Munich in 1913, the Budapest local group was formed under the chairmanship of Ferenczi. Soon after this the first English group was formed by Ernest Jones, who had returned to London. The membership of these local groups, of which there were now eight, naturally affords no means of estimating the number of unorganized students and adherents of psycho-analysis.

The development of the periodicals devoted to psychoanalysis also deserves a brief mention. The first of these was a series of monographs entitled *Schriften zur angewandten Seelenkunde* ['Papers on Applied Mental Science'][1] which have appeared irregularly since 1907 and now number fifteen issues. (The publisher was to begin with Heller in Vienna and later F. Deuticke.) They comprise works by Freud (Nos. 1 and 7), Riklin, Jung, Abraham (Nos. 4 and 11), Rank (Nos. 5 and 13), Sadger, Pfister, Max Graf, Jones (Nos. 10 and 14), Storfer and von Hug-Hellmuth.[2] When the journal *Imago* (which will be referred to shortly [p. 47]) was founded, this form of publication ceased to have quite the same value. After the meeting at Salzburg in 1908, the *Jahrbuch für psychoanalytische und psychopathologische Forschungen* [*Yearbook for Psycho-Analytic and Psychopathological Researches*] was founded, which appeared for five years under Jung's editorship and has now re-emerged, under two new editors [3] and with a slight change in its title, as the *Jahrbuch der Psychoanalyse* [*Yearbook of Psycho-Analysis*.] It is no

---

[1] [See Freud's prospectus for that series (1907*e*).]

[2] [*Footnote added* 1924:] Since then, further works have appeared, by Sadger (Nos. 16 and 18) and Kielholz (No. 17).

[3] [See above p. 7 *n*.]

longer intended to be, as it has been in recent years, merely a repository for the publication of self-contained works. Instead, it will endeavour, through the activity of its editors, to fulfil the aim of recording all the work done and all the advances made in the sphere of psycho-analysis.[1] The *Zentralblatt für Psychoanalyse*, which, as I have already said, was started by Adler and Stekel after the foundation of the International Psycho-Analytical Association in Nuremberg in 1910, has, during its short existence, had a stormy career. As early as in the tenth number of the first volume [July, 1911] an announcement appeared on the front page that, on account of scientific differences of opinion with the director, Dr. Alfred Adler had decided to withdraw voluntarily from the editorship. After this Dr. Stekel remained the only editor (from the summer of 1911). At the Weimar Congress [September, 1911] the *Zentralblatt* was raised to the position of official organ of the International Association and made available to all members in return for an increase in the annual subscription. From the third number of the second volume[2] onwards (winter [December], 1912) Stekel became solely responsible for its contents. His behaviour, of which it is not easy to publish an account, had compelled me to resign the direction and hurriedly to establish a new organ for psycho-analysis—the *Internationale Zeitschrift für ärztliche Psychoanalyse* [*International Journal for Medical Psycho-Analysis*]. The combined efforts of almost all our workers and of Hugo Heller, the new publisher, resulted in the appearance of the first number in January, 1913, whereupon it took the place of the *Zentralblatt* as official organ of the International Psycho-Analytical Association.

Meanwhile, early in 1912, a new periodical, *Imago* (published by Heller), designed exclusively for the application of psychoanalysis to the mental sciences, was founded by Dr. Hanns Sachs and Dr. Otto Rank. *Imago* is now in the middle of its third volume and is read with interest by a continually increasing number of subscribers, some of whom have little connection with medical analysis.[3]

[1] [*Footnote added* 1924:] It ceased publication at the beginning of the War [after only a single volume (1914) had been issued].

[2] ['Second volume' in all former editions. It should in fact be '*third* volume'. The volumes ran from October to September.]

[3] [*Footnote added* 1924:] The publication of these two periodicals was transferred in 1919 to the Internationaler Psychoanalytischer Verlag [the

Apart from these four periodical publications (*Schriften zur angewandten Seelenkunde*, *Jahrbuch*, *Zeitschrift* and *Imago*) other German and foreign journals publish works which may claim a place in the literature of psycho-analysis. *The Journal of Abnormal Psychology*, directed by Morton Prince, usually contains so many good analytic contributions that it must be regarded as the principal representative of analytic literature in America. In the winter of 1913, White and Jelliffe in New York started a new periodical (*The Psychoanalytic Review*) which is devoted exclusively to psycho-analysis, no doubt bearing in mind the fact that most medical men in America who are interested in analysis find the German language a difficulty.[1]

I must now mention two secessions which have taken place among the adherents of psycho-analysis; the first occurred between the founding of the Association in 1910 and the Weimar Congress in 1911; the second took place after this and became manifest at Munich in 1913. The disappointment that they caused me might have been averted if I had paid more attention to the reactions of patients under analytic treatment. I knew very well of course that anyone may take to flight at his first approach to the unwelcome truths of analysis; I had always myself maintained that everyone's understanding of it is limited by his own repressions (or rather, by the resistances which sustain them) so that he cannot go beyond a particular point in his relation to analysis. But I had not expected that anyone who had reached a certain depth in his understanding of analysis could renounce that understanding and lose it. And yet daily experience with patients had shown that total rejection of analytic knowledge may result whenever a specially strong resistance arises at any depth in the mind; one may have

International Psycho-Analytical Publishing House]. At the present time (1923) they are both in their ninth volume. (Actually, the *Internationale Zeitschrift* is in the eleventh and *Imago* in the twelfth year of its existence, but, in consequence of events during the war, Volume IV of the *Zeitschrift* covered more than one year, i.e. the years 1916–18, and Volume V of *Imago* the years 1917–18.) With the beginning of Volume VI the word '*ärztliche*' ['medical'] was dropped from the title of the *Internationale Zeitschrift*.

[1] [*Footnote added* 1924:] In 1920 Ernest Jones undertook the founding of *The International Journal of Psycho-Analysis*, intended for readers in England and America.

succeeded in laboriously bringing a patient to grasp some parts of analytic knowledge and to handle them like possessions of his own, and yet one may see him, under the domination of the very next resistance, throw all he has learnt to the winds and stand on the defensive as he did in the days when he was a carefree beginner. I had to learn that the very same thing can happen with psycho-analysts as with patients in analysis.

It is no easy or enviable task to write the history of these two secessions, partly because I am without any strong personal motive for doing so—I had not expected gratitude nor am I revengeful to any effective degree—and partly because I know that by doing so I shall lay myself open to the invectives of my not too scrupulous opponents and offer the enemies of analysis the spectacle they so heartily desire—of 'the psycho-analysts tearing one another limb from limb'. After exercising so much self-restraint in not coming to blows with opponents outside analysis, I now see myself compelled to take up arms against its former followers or people who still like to call themselves its followers. I have no choice in the matter, however; only indolence or cowardice could lead one to keep silence, and silence would cause more harm than a frank revelation of the harms that already exist. Anyone who has followed the growth of other scientific movements will know that the same upheavals and dissensions commonly occur in them as well. It may be that elsewhere they are more carefully concealed; but psycho-analysis, which repudiates so many conventional ideals, is more honest in these matters too.

Another very severe drawback is that I cannot entirely avoid throwing some analytic light on these two opposition movements. Analysis is not suited, however, for polemical use; it presupposes the consent of the person who is being analysed and a situation in which there is a superior and a subordinate. Anyone, therefore, who undertakes an analysis for polemical purposes must expect the person analysed to use analysis against him in turn, so that the discussion will reach a state which entirely excludes the possibility of convincing any impartial third person. I shall therefore restrict to a minimum my use of analytic knowledge, and, with it, of indiscretion and aggressiveness towards my opponents; and I may also point out that I am not basing any scientific criticism on these grounds. I am not concerned with the truth that may be contained in the theories which I am rejecting, nor shall I attempt to refute them. I shall leave that task to other qualified workers in the field of psycho-analysis, and it has, indeed, already been partly accomplished. I wish merely to show that these theories controvert the fundamental principles of analysis (and on what points they controvert them) and that for this reason they should not be known by the name of analysis. So I shall avail myself of analysis only in order to explain how these divergences from it could arise among analysts. When I come to the points at which the divergences occurred, I shall have, it is true, to defend the just rights of psycho-analysis with some remarks of a purely critical nature.

The first task confronting psycho-analysis was to explain the neuroses; it used the two facts of resistance and transference as starting-points, and, taking into consideration the third fact of amnesia, accounted for them with its theories of repression, of the sexual motive forces in neurosis and of the unconscious. Psycho-analysis has never claimed to provide a complete theory of human mentality in general, but only expected that what it offered should be applied to supplement and correct the knowledge acquired by other means. Adler's theory, however, goes far beyond this point; it seeks at one stroke to explain the behaviour and character of human beings as well as their neurotic and psychotic illnesses. It is actually more suited to any other field than that of neurosis, although for reasons connected with the history of its development it still places this in the foreground. For many years I had opportunities of studying Dr. Adler and have never refused to recognize his unusual ability, combined with a particularly speculative disposition. As an instance of the 'persecution' to which he asserts he has been subjected by me, I can point to the fact that after the Association was founded I made over to him the leadership of the Vienna group. It was not until urgent demands were put forward by all the members of the society that I let myself be persuaded to take the chair again at its scientific meetings. When I perceived how little gift Adler had precisely for judging unconscious material, my view changed to an expectation that he would succeed in discovering the connections of psycho-analysis with psychology and with the biological foundations of instinctual processes—an expectation which was in some sense justified by the valuable work he had done on 'organ-inferiority'.[1] And he did in fact effect something of the kind; but his work conveys an impression 'as if'—to speak in his own 'jargon'[2]—it was intended to prove that psycho-analysis was wrong in everything and that it had only attributed so much importance to sexual motive forces because of its credulity in accepting the assertions of neurotics. I may even speak publicly of the personal motive for his work, since he himself announced it in the presence of a small circle of members of the Vienna group:—'Do you think it gives me such great pleasure to stand in your shadow my whole life long?' To be sure, I see nothing reprehensible in a younger man freely admitting his ambition, which one would in any case guess was among the incentives for his work. But even though a man is dominated by a motive of this kind he should know how to avoid being what the English, with their fine social tact, call 'unfair'—which in German can only be expressed by a much cruder word. How little Adler has succeeded in this is shown by the profusion of petty outbursts of malice which disfigure his writings and by the indications they contain of an uncontrolled craving for priority. At the Vienna Psycho-Analytical Society we once actually heard him claim priority for the conception of the 'unity of the neuroses' and for the 'dynamic view' of them. This came as a great surprise to me, for I had always believed that these two principles were stated by me before I ever made Adler's acquaintance.

This striving of Adler's for a place in the sun has, however, had one result which is bound to be beneficial to psycho-analysis. When, after irreconcilable scientific disagreements had come to light, I was obliged to bring about Adler's resignation from the editorship of the *Zentralblatt*, he left the Vienna society as well, and founded a new one, which at first adopted the tasteful name of 'The Society for Free Psycho-Analysis' ['*Verein für freie Psychoanalyse*']. But outsiders who are unconnected with analysis are evidently as unskilful in appreciating the differences between the views of two psycho-analysts as we Europeans are in detecting the differences between two Chinese faces. 'Free' psycho-analysis remained in the shadow of 'official', 'orthodox' psycho-analysis and was treated merely as an appendage to the

[1] [Adler, 1907.]
[2] [The terms 'as if' and 'jargon' figure prominently in Adler's writings.]

latter. Then Adler took a step for which we are thankful; he severed all connection with psycho-analysis, and gave his theory the name of 'Individual Psychology'. There is room enough on God's earth, and anyone who can has a perfect right to potter about on it without being prevented; but it is not a desirable thing for people who have ceased to understand one another and have grown incompatible with one another to remain under the same roof. Adler's 'Individual Psychology' is now one of the many schools of psychology which are adverse to psycho-analysis and its further development is no concern of ours.

The Adlerian theory was from the very beginning a 'system'— which psycho-analysis was careful to avoid becoming. It is also a remarkably good example of 'secondary revision', such as occurs, for instance, in the process to which dream-material is submitted by the action of waking thought. In Adler's case the place of dream-material is taken by the new material obtained through psycho-analytic studies; this is then viewed purely from the standpoint of the ego, reduced to the categories with which the ego is familiar, translated, twisted and—exactly as happens in dream-formation—is misunderstood.[1] Moreover, the Adlerian theory is characterized less by what it asserts than by what it denies, so that it consists of three sorts of elements of quite dissimilar value: useful contributions to the psychology of the ego, superfluous but admissible translations of the analytic facts into the new 'jargon', and distortions and perversions of these facts when they do not comply with the requirements of the ego.

The elements of the first sort have never been ignored by psycho-analysis, although they did not deserve any special attention from it; it was more concerned to show that every ego-trend contains libidinal components. The Adlerian theory emphasizes the counterpart to this, the egoistic constituent in libidinal instinctual impulses. This would have been an appreciable gain if Adler had not on every occasion used this observation in order to deny the libidinal impulses in favour of their egoistic instinctual components. His theory does what every patient does and what our conscious thought in general does— namely, makes use of a *rationalization*, as Jones [1908] has called it, in order to conceal the unconscious motive. Adler is so

[1] [See Chapter VI (I) of *The Interpretation of Dreams*.]

consistent in this that he positively considers that the strongest motive force in the sexual act is the man's intention of showing himself master of the woman—of being 'on top'. I do not know if he has expressed these monstrous notions in his writings.

Psycho-analysis recognized early that every neurotic symptom owes its possibility of existence to a compromise. Every symptom must therefore in some way comply with the demands of the ego which manipulates the repression; it must offer some advantage, it must admit of some useful application, or it would meet with the same fate as the original instinctual impulse itself which has been fended off. The term 'gain from illness' has taken this into account; one is even justified in differentiating the 'primary' gain to the ego, which must be operative at the time of the generation of the symptom, from a 'secondary' part, which supervenes in attachment to other purposes of the ego, if the symptom is to persist.[1] It has also long been known that the withdrawal of this gain from illness, or its disappearance in consequence of some change in real external circumstances, constitutes one of the mechanisms of a cure of the symptom. In the Adlerian doctrine the main emphasis falls on these easily verifiable and clearly intelligible connections, while the fact is altogether overlooked that on countless occasions the ego is merely making a virtue of necessity in submitting, because of its usefulness, to the very disagreeable symptom which is forced upon it—for instance, in accepting anxiety as a means to security. The ego is here playing the ludicrous part of the clown in a circus who by his gestures tries to convince the audience that every change in the circus ring is being carried out under his orders. But only the youngest of the spectators are deceived by him.

Psycho-analysis is obliged to give its backing to the second constituent of Adler's theory as it would to something of its own, And in fact it is nothing else than psycho-analytic knowledge. which that author extracted from sources open to everyone during ten years of work in common and which he has now labelled as his own by a change in nomenclature. I myself consider 'safeguarding [*Sicherung*]', for instance, a better term than 'protective measure [*Schutzmassregel*]' which is the one I employ; but I cannot discover any difference in their meaning. Again, a

[1] [A full discussion of the primary and secondary gain from illness will be found in Lecture XXIV of Freud's *Introductory Lectures* (1916–17).]

host of familiar features come to light in Adler's propositions when one restores the earlier 'phantasied' and 'phantasy' in place of 'feigned [*fingiert*]', 'fictive' and 'fiction'. The identity of these terms would be insisted upon by psycho-analysis even if their author had not taken part in our common work over a period of many years.

The third part of the Adlerian theory, the twisted interpretations and distortions of the disagreeable facts of analysis, are what definitely separate 'Individual Psychology', as it is now to be called, from psycho-analysis. As we know, the principle of Adler's system is that the individual's aim of self-assertion, his 'will to power', is what, in the form of a 'masculine protest',[1] plays a dominating part in the conduct of life, in character-formation and in neurosis. This 'masculine protest', the Adlerian motive force, is nothing else, however, but repression detached from its psychological mechanism and, moreover, sexualized in addition—which ill accords with the vaunted ejection of sexuality from its place in mental life.[2] The 'masculine protest' undoubtedly exists, but if it is made into the [sole] motive force of mental life the observed facts are being treated like a spring-board that is left behind after it has been used to jump off from. Let us consider one of the fundamental situations in which desire is felt in infancy: that of a child observing the sexual act between adults. Analysis shows, in the case of people with whose life-story the physician will later be concerned, that at such moments two impulses take possession of the immature spectator. In boys, one is the impulse to put himself in the place of the active man, and the other, the opposing current, is the impulse to identify himself with the passive woman.[3] Between them these two impulses exhaust the pleasurable possibilities of the situation. The first alone can come under

[1] [The term 'masculine protest' was introduced by Adler in a paper 'Der psychische Hermaphroditismus im Leben und in der Neurose [Psychical Hermaphroditism in Life and in Neurosis]' at the Nuremberg International Psycho-Analytical Congress in 1910. An abstract appeared in *Jb. psychoan. psychopath. Forsch.*, **2** (1910), 738, and the paper was published in full in *Fortschritte der Medizin*, **28** (1910), 486.]

[2] [Freud discussed Adler's explanation of repression at greater length at the end of his paper 'A Child is Being Beaten' (1919*e*).

[3] [Cf. Chapter III of *The Ego and the Id* (1923*b*), (Norton, 1960).]

the head of the masculine protest, if that concept is to retain any meaning at all. The second, however, the further course of which Adler disregards or which he knows nothing about, is the one that will become the more important in the subsequent neurosis. Adler has so merged himself in the jealous narrowness of the ego that he takes account only of those instinctual impulses which are agreeable to the ego and are encouraged by it; the situation in neurosis, in which the impulses are *opposed* to the ego, is precisely the one that lies beyond his horizon.

In connection with the attempt, which psycho-analysis has made necessary, to correlate the fundamental principle of its theory with the mental life of children, Adler exhibits the most serious departures from actual observation and the most fundamental confusion in his concepts. The biological, social and psychological meanings of 'masculine' and 'feminine' are here hopelessly mixed.[1] It is impossible, and is disproved by observation, that a child, whether male or female, should found the plan of its life on an original depreciation of the female sex and take the wish to be a real man as its 'guiding line'.[2] Children have, to begin with, no idea of the significance of the distinction between the sexes; on the contrary, they start with the assumption that the same genital organ (the male one) is possessed by both sexes; they do not begin their sexual researches with the problem of the distinction between the sexes,[3] while the *social* underestimation of women is completely foreign to them. There are women in whose neurosis the wish to be a man has played no part. Whatever in the nature of a masculine protest can be shown to exist is easily traceable to a disturbance in primary narcissism due to threats of castration or to the earliest interferences with sexual activities. All disputes about the psychogenesis of the neuroses must eventually be decided in the field of the neuroses of childhood. Careful dissection of a neurosis in early childhood puts an end to all misapprehensions about the

[1] [Cf. a footnote added in 1915 to Section 4 of the third of Freud's *Three Essays* (1905d).]

[2] ['*Leitlinie*', a term constantly used by Adler.]

[3] [This statement (which was repeated in a passage added in 1915 to Section 5 of the second of Freud's *Three Essays*, was corrected in his later paper on the distinction between the sexes (1925j).]

aetiology of the neuroses and to all doubts about the part played by the sexual instincts in them.[1] That is why, in his criticism of Jung's paper 'Conflicts in the Mind of the Child' [1910c], Adler [1911a] was obliged to resort to the imputation that the facts of the case had been one-sidedly arranged, 'no doubt by the [child's] father'.

I will not dwell any longer on the biological aspect of the Adlerian theory nor discuss whether either actual 'organ-inferiority' [p. 51 n.1] or the subjective feeling of it—one does not know which—is really capable of serving as the foundation of Adler's system. I will merely remark in passing that if it were so neurosis would appear as a by-product of every kind of physical decrepitude, whereas observation shows that an impressive majority of ugly, misshapen, crippled and miserable people fail to react to their defects by neurosis. Nor will I deal with the interesting assertion according to which inferiority is to be traced back to the feeling of being a child. It shows the disguise under which the factor of infantilism, which is so strongly emphasized by psycho-analysis, re-appears in 'Individual Psychology'. On the other hand, I must point out how all the psychological acquisitions of psycho-analysis have been thrown to the winds by Adler. In his book *Über den nervösen Charakter* [1912] the unconscious is still mentioned as a psychological peculiarity, without, however, any relation to his system. Later, he has consistently declared that it is a matter of indifference to him whether an idea is conscious or unconscious. Adler has never from the first shown any understanding of repression. In an abstract of a paper read by him at the Vienna Society (February, 1911) he wrote that it must be pointed out that the evidence in a particular case showed that the patient had never repressed his libido, but had been continually 'safeguarding' himself against it.[2] Soon afterwards, in a discussion at the Vienna Society, he said: 'If you ask where repression comes from, you are told, "from civilization"; but if you go on to ask where civilization comes from, you are told "from repression". So you see it is all simply playing with words.' A tithe of the acuteness and ingenuity with which Adler has unmasked the

---

[1] [The illustration of this fact is the main thesis of Freud's 'Wolf Man' analysis (1918b), which was drafted a few months after the present paper.]

[2] [This abstract will be found in *Zbl. Psychoan.*, **1**, 371.]

defensive devices of the 'nervous character' would have been enough to show him the way out of this pettifogging argument. What is meant is simply that civilization is based on the repressions effected by former generations, and that each fresh generation is required to maintain this civilization by effecting the same repressions. I once heard of a child who thought people were laughing at him, and began to cry, because when he asked where eggs come from he was told 'from hens', and when he went on to ask where hens come from he was told 'from eggs'. But they were not playing with words; on the contrary, they were telling him the truth.

Everything that Adler has to say about dreams, the shibboleth of psycho-analysis, is equally empty and unmeaning. At first he regarded dreams as a turning away from the feminine to the masculine line—which is simply a translation of the wish-fulfilment theory of dreams into the language of the 'masculine protest'. Later he found that the essence of dreams lies in enabling men to accomplish unconsciously what they are denied consciously. Adler [1911b, 215 n.] must also be credited with priority in confusing dreams with latent dream-thoughts—a confusion on which the discovery of his 'prospective tendency' rests. Maeder [1912] followed his lead in this later.[1] Here the fact is readily overlooked that every interpretation of a dream which is incomprehensible in its manifest form is based on the very method of dream-interpretation whose premisses and conclusions are being disputed. In regard to resistance Adler informs us that it serves the purpose of putting into effect the patient's opposition to the physician. This is certainly true; it is as much as to say that it serves the purpose of resistance. Where it comes from, however, or how it happens that its phenomena are at the disposal of the patient is not further enquired into, as being of no interest to the ego. The detailed mechanism of the symptoms and manifestations of diseases, the explanation of the manifold variety of those diseases and their forms of expression, are disregarded *in toto*; for everything alike is pressed into the service of the masculine protest, self-assertion and the aggrandizement o fthe personality. The system is complete; to produce it has cost an enormous amount of labour in the re-casting of interpretations, while it has not furnished a single new

[1] [See a footnote added in 1914 to Chapter VII (D) of *The Interpretation of Dreams*.]

observation. I fancy I have made it clear that it has nothing to do with psycho-analysis.

The view of life which is reflected in the Adlerian system is founded exclusively on the aggressive instinct; there is no room in it for love. We might feel surprise that such a cheerless *Weltanschauung* should have met with any attention at all; but we must not forget that human beings, weighed down by the burden of their sexual needs, are ready to accept any thing if only the 'overcoming of sexuality' is offered them as a bait.

Adler's secession took place before the Weimar Congress in 1911; after that date the Swiss began theirs. The first signs of it, curiously enough, were a few remarks of Riklin's in some popular articles appearing in Swiss publications, so that the general public learned earlier than those most intimately concerned in the subject that psycho-analysis had got the better of some regrettable errors which had previously discredited it. In 1912 Jung boasted, in a letter from America, that his modifications of psycho-analysis had overcome the resistances of many people who had hitherto refused to have anything to do with it. I replied that that was nothing to boast of, and that the more he sacrificed of the hard-won truths of psycho-analysis the more would he see resistances vanishing. This modification which the Swiss were so proud of introducing was again nothing else but a pushing into the background of the sexual factor in psycho-analytic theory. I confess that from the beginning I regarded this 'advance' as too far-reaching an adjustment to the demands of actuality.

These two retrograde movements away from psycho-analysis, which I must now compare with each other, show another point in common: for they both court a favourable opinion by putting forward certain lofty ideas, which view things, as it were, *sub specie aeternitatis*. With Adler, this part is played by the relativity of all knowledge and the right of the personality to put an artificial construction on the data of knowledge according to individual taste; with Jung, the appeal is made to the historic right of youth to throw off the fetters in which tyrannical age with its hidebound views seeks to bind it. A few words must be devoted to exposing the fallacy of these ideas.

The relativity of our knowledge is a consideration which may be advanced against every other science just as well as against psycho-analysis. It is derived from familiar reactionary currents of present-day feeling which are hostile to science, and it lays claim to an appearance of superiority to which no one is entitled. None of us can guess what the ultimate judgement of mankind about our theoretical efforts will be. There are instances in which rejection by the first three generations has been corrected by the succeeding one and changed into recognition. After a man has listened carefully to the voice of criticism in himself and has paid some attention to the criticisms of his opponents, there is nothing for him to do but with all his strength to maintain his own convictions which are based on experience. One should be content to conduct one's case honestly, and should not assume the office of judge, which is reserved for the remote future. The stress on arbitrary personal views in scientific matters is bad; it is clearly an attempt to dispute the right of psycho-analysis to be valued as a science —after that value, incidentally, has already been depreciated by what has been said before [on the relative nature of all knowledge]. Anyone who sets a high value on scientific thought will rather seek every possible means and method of circumscribing the factor of fanciful personal predilections as far as possible wherever it still plays too great a part. Moreover, it is opportune to recall that any zeal in defending ourselves is out of place. These arguments of Adler's are not intended seriously. They are only meant for use against his opponents; they do not touch his own theories. Nor have they prevented his followers from hailing him as the Messiah, for whose appearance expectant humanity has been prepared by a number of forerunners. The Messiah is certainly no relative phenomenon.

Jung's argument *ad captandam benevolentiam*[1] rests on the too optimistic assumption that the progress of the human race, of civilization and knowledge, has always pursued an unbroken line; as if there had been no periods of decadence, no reactions and restorations after every revolution, no generations who have taken a backward step and abandoned the gains of their predecessors. His approach to the standpoint of the masses, his abandonment of an innovation which proved unwelcome, make it *a priori* improbable that Jung's corrected version of psycho-analysis can justly claim to be a youthful act of liberation. After

[1] ['For the purpose of gaining good-will.']

all, it is not the age of the doer that decides this but the character of the deed.

Of the two movements under discussion Adler's is indubitably the more important; while radically false, it is marked by consistency and coherence. It is, moreover, in spite of everything, founded upon a theory of the instincts. Jung's modification, on the other hand, loosens the connection of the phenomena with instinctual life; and further, as its critics (e.g. Abraham, Ferenczi and Jones) have pointed out, it is so obscure, unintelligible and confused as to make it difficult to take up any position upon it. Wherever one lays hold of anything, one must be prepared to hear that one has misunderstood it, and one cannot see how to arrive at a correct understanding of it. It is put forward in a peculiarly vacillating manner, one moment as 'quite a mild deviation, which does not justify the outcry that has been raised about it' (Jung), and the next moment as a new message of salvation which is to begin a new epoch for psycho-analysis, and, indeed, a new *Weltanschauung* for everyone.

When one thinks of the inconsistencies displayed in the various public and private pronouncements made by the Jungian movement, one is bound to ask oneself how much of this is due to lack of clearness and how much to lack of sincerity. It must be admitted, however, that the exponents of the new theory find themselves in a difficult position. They are now disputing things which they themselves formerly upheld, and they are doing so, moreover, not on the ground of fresh observations which might have taught them something further, but in consequence of fresh interpretations which make the things they see look different to them now from what they did before. For this reason they are unwilling to give up their connection with psycho-analysis, as whose representatives they became known to the world, and prefer to give it out that psycho-analysis has changed. At the Munich Congress I found it necessary to clear up this confusion, and I did so by declaring that I did not recognize the innovations of the Swiss as legitimate continuations and further developments of the psycho-analysis that originated with me. Outside critics (like Furtmüller) had already seen how things were, and Abraham is right in saying that Jung is in full retreat from psycho-analysis. I am of course perfectly ready to allow that everyone has a right to think and to write what he pleases; but he has no right to put it forward as something other than what it really is.

Just as Adler's investigation brought something new to psycho-analysis—a contribution to the psychology of the ego—and then expected us to pay too high a price for this gift by throwing over all the fundamental theories of analysis, so in the same way Jung and his followers paved the way for their fight against psycho-analysis by presenting it with a new acquisition. They traced in detail (as Pfister did before them) the way in which the material of sexual ideas belonging to the family-complex and incestuous object-choice is made use of in repre-senting the highest ethical and religious interests of man—that is, they have illuminated an important instance of the sublima-tion of the erotic instinctual forces and of their transformation into trends which can no longer be called erotic. This was in complete harmony with all the expectations of psycho-analysis, and would have agreed very well with the view that in dreams and neurosis a regressive dissolution of this sublimation, as of all others, becomes visible. But the world would have risen in indignation and protested that ethics and religion were being sexualized. Now I cannot refrain from thinking teleologically for once and concluding that these discoverers were not equal to meeting such a storm of indignation. Perhaps it even began to rage in their own bosoms. The theological prehistory of so many of the Swiss throws no less light on their attitude to psycho-analysis than does Adler's socialist prehistory on the development of his psychology. One is reminded of Mark Twain's famous story of all the things that happened to his watch and of his concluding words: 'And he used to wonder what became of all the unsuccessful tinkers, and gunsmiths, and shoemakers, and blacksmiths; but nobody could ever tell him.'

Suppose—to make use of a simile—that in a particular social group there lives a *parvenu*, who boasts of being descended from a noble family living in another place. It is pointed out to him, however, that his parents live somewhere in the neighbourhood, and that they are quite humble people. There is only one way of escape from his difficulty and he seizes on it. He can no longer repudiate his parents, but he asserts that they themselves are of noble lineage and have merely come down in the world; and he procures a family-tree from some obliging official source. It seems to me that the Swiss have been obliged to behave in much the same way. If ethics and religion were not allowed to be sexualized but had to be something 'higher' from the start, and if nevertheless the ideas contained in them seemed undeniably to be descended from the Oedipus and family-complex, there could be only one way out: it must be that from the very first these complexes themselves do not mean what they seem to be expressing, but bear the higher 'anagogic' meaning (as Silberer calls it) which made it possible for them to be employed in the abstract trains of thought of ethics and religious mysticism.

I am quite prepared to be told again that I have misunderstood the substance and purpose of the Neo-Zurich theory; but I must protest in advance against any contradictions to my view of it that may be found in the publications of that school being laid at my door instead of theirs. I can find no other way of making the whole range of Jung's innovations intelligible to myself and of grasping all their implications. All the changes that Jung has proposed to make in psycho-analysis flow from his intention to eliminate what is objectionable in the family-complexes, so as not to find it again in religion and ethics. For sexual libido an abstract concept has been substituted, of which one may safely say that it remains mystifying and incomprehensible to wise men and fools alike. The Oedipus complex has a merely 'symbolic' meaning: the mother in it means the unattainable, which must be renounced in the interests of civilization; the father who is killed in the Oedipus myth is the 'inner' father, from whom one must set oneself free in order to become independent. Other parts of the material of sexual ideas will no doubt be subjected to similar re-interpretations in the course of time. In the place of a conflict between ego-dystonic erotic trends and the self-preservative ones a conflict appears between the 'life-task' and 'psychical inertia' [p. 272]; the neurotic's sense of guilt corresponds to his self-reproach for not properly fulfilling his 'life-task'. In this way a new religio-ethical system has been created, which, just like the Adlerian system, was bound to re-interpret, distort or jettison the factual findings of analysis. The truth is that these people have picked out a few cultural overtones from the symphony of life and have once more failed to hear the mighty and primordial melody of the instincts.

In order to preserve this system intact it was necessary to turn entirely away from observation and from the technique of psycho-analysis. Occasionally enthusiasm for the cause even permitted a disregard of scientific logic—as when Jung finds that the Oedipus complex is not 'specific' enough for the aetiology of the neuroses, and proceeds to attribute this specific quality to inertia, the most universal characteristic of all matter, animate and inanimate! It is to be noted, by the way, that the 'Oedipus complex' represents only a topic with which the individual's mental forces have to deal, and is not itself a force, like 'psychical inertia'. The study of individual people had shown (and always will show) that the sexual complexes in their original sense are alive in them. On that account the investigation of individuals was pushed into the background [in the new theories] and replaced by conclusions based on evidence derived from anthropological research. The greatest risk of coming up against the original, undisguised meaning of these re-interpreted complexes was to be met with in the early childhood of every individual; consequently in therapy the injunction was laid down that this past history should be dwelt on as little as possible and the main emphasis put on reverting to the current conflict, in which, moreover, the essential thing was on no account to be what was accidental and personal, but what was general—in fact, the non-fulfilment of the life-task. As we know, however, a neurotic's current conflict becomes comprehensible and admits of solution only when it is traced back to his prehistory, when one goes back along the path that his libido took when he fell ill.

The form taken by the Neo-Zurich therapy under these influences can be conveyed in the words of a patient who experienced it himself: 'This time not a trace of attention was given to the past or to the transference. Wherever I thought I recognized the latter it was pronounced to be a pure libidinal symbol. The moral instruction was very fine and I followed it faithfully, but I did not advance a step. It was even more annoying for me than for him, but how could I help it? . . . Instead of freeing me by analysis, every day brought fresh tremendous demands on me, which had to be fulfilled if the neurosis was to be conquered—for instance, inward concentration by means of introversion, religious meditation, resuming life with my wife in loving devotion, etc. It was almost beyond one's strength; it was aiming at a radical transformation of one's whole inner nature. I left the analysis as a poor sinner with intense feelings of contrition and the best resolutions, but at the same time in utter discouragement. Any clergyman would have advised what he recommended, but where was I to find the strength?' The patient, it is true, reported that he had heard that analysis of the past and of the transference must be gone through first; but he had been told that he had already had enough of it. Since this first kind of analysis had not helped him more, the conclusion seems to me justified that the patient had *not* had enough of it. Certainly the subsequent treatment, which no longer had any claim to be called psycho-analysis, did not improve matters. It is remarkable that the members of the Zurich school should have made the long journey round by way of Vienna in order to wind up at the nearby city of Berne, where Dubois[1] cures neuroses by ethical encouragement in a more considerate manner.[2]

The total incompatibility of this new movement with psycho-analysis shows itself too, of course, in Jung's treatment of repression, which is hardly mentioned nowadays in his writings, in his misunderstanding of dreams, which, like Adler [cf. p. 57], in complete disregard of dream-psychology, he confuses with the latent dream-thoughts, and in his loss of all understanding of the unconscious—in short, in all the points which I should regard as the essence of psycho-analysis. When Jung tells us that the incest-complex is merely 'symbolic', that after all it has no 'real' existence, that after all a savage feels no desire towards an old hag but prefers a young and pretty woman, we are tempted to conclude that 'symbolic' and 'without real existence' simply mean something which, in virtue of its manifestations and pathogenic effects, is described by psycho-analysis as 'existing unconsciously'—a description that disposes of the apparent contradiction.

If one bears in mind that dreams are something different from the latent dream-thoughts which they work over, there is

---

[1] [Paul Dubois (1848–1918), Professor of Neuropathology at Berne, had some celebrity during the early part of the century for his method of treating neuroses by 'persuasion'.]

[2] I know the objections there are to making use of a patient's reports, and I will therefore expressly state that my informant is a trustworthy person, very well capable of forming a judgement. He gave me this information quite spontaneously and I make use of his communication without asking his consent, since I cannot allow that a psycho-analytic technique has any right to claim the protection of medical discretion.

nothing surprising in patients dreaming of things with which their minds have been filled during the treatment, whether it be the 'life-task', or 'being on top' or 'underneath'. The dreams of people being analysed can undoubtedly be directed, in the same way as they are by stimuli produced for experimental purposes. One can determine a part of the material which appears in a dream; nothing in the essence or mechanism of dreams is altered by this. Nor do I believe that 'biographical' dreams, as they are called, occur outside analysis.¹ If, on the other hand, one analyses dreams which occurred before treatment, or if one considers the dreamer's own additions to what has been suggested to him in the treatment, or if one avoids setting him any such tasks, then one may convince oneself how far removed it is from the purpose of a dream to produce attempted solutions of the life-task. Dreams are only a form of thinking; one can never reach an understanding of this form by reference to the content of the thoughts; only an appreciation of the dream-work will lead to that understanding.²

It is not difficult to find a factual refutation of Jung's misconceptions of psycho-analysis and deviations from it. Every analysis conducted in a proper manner, and in particular every analysis of a child, strengthens the convictions upon which the theory of psycho-analysis is founded, and rebuts the re-interpretations made by both Jung's and Adler's systems. In the days before his illumination, Jung himself [1910b, see above p. 31] carried out and published an analysis of this kind of a child; it remains to be seen whether he will undertake a new interpretation of its results with the help of a different 'one-sided arrangement of the facts', to use the expression employed by Adler in this connection [p. 56 above].

The view that the sexual representation of 'higher' thoughts in dreams and neurosis is nothing but an archaic mode of expression is of course irreconcilable with the fact that in neurosis these sexual complexes prove to be the bearers of the quantities of libido which have been withdrawn from utilization in real life. If it was merely a question of a sexual 'jargon', the

¹ [See a sentence added in 1925 near the end of Chapter VI (D) of *The Interpretation of Dreams*.]

² [The topic of this paragraph was discussed by Freud at greater length in Section VII of 'Remarks on the Theory and Practice of Dream-Interpretation' (1923c). Cf. also a footnote added in 1925 to Chapter VI (I) of *The Interpretation of Dreams*.]

economy of the libido could not have been altered in any way by it. Jung admits this himself in his *Darstellung der psychoanalytischen Theorie* [1913] and formulates the task of therapy as the detaching of libidinal cathexes from these complexes. This can never be achieved, however, by directing the patient away from them and urging him to sublimate, but only by exhaustive examination of them and by making them fully and completely conscious. The first piece of reality which the patient must deal with is his illness. Efforts to spare him that task point to the physician's incapacity to help him to overcome his resistances, or else to the physician's dread of the results of the work.

It may be said lastly that by his 'modification' of psychoanalysis Jung has given us a counterpart to the famous Lichtenberg knife.[1] He has changed the hilt, and he has put a new blade into it; yet because the same name is engraved on it we are expected to regard the instrument as the original one.

I think I have made clear, on the contrary, that the new teaching which aims at replacing psycho-analysis signifies an abandonment of analysis and a secession from it. Some people may be inclined to fear that this secession is bound to have more momentous consequences for analysis than would another, owing to its having been started by men who have played so great a part in the movement and have done so much to advance it. I do not share this apprehension.

Men are strong so long as they represent a strong idea; they become powerless when they oppose it. Psycho-analysis will survive this loss and gain new adherents in place of these. In conclusion, I can only express a wish that fortune may grant an agreeable upward journey to all those who have found their stay in the underworld of psycho-analysis too uncomfortable for their taste. The rest of us, I hope, will be permitted without hindrance to carry through to their conclusion our labours in the depths.

February, 1914.

[1] [The *mot* is quoted in a footnote to Section 8 of Chapter II of Freud's book on jokes (1905c).]

BIBLIOGRAPHY
AND AUTHOR INDEX

[Titles of books and periodicals are in italics; titles of papers are in inverted commas. Abbreviations are in accordance with the *World List of Scientific Periodicals* (London, 1952). Further abbreviations used in this volume will be found in the List at the end of this bibliography. Numerals in thick type refer to volumes; ordinary numerals refer to pages. The figures in round brackets at the end of each entry indicate the page or pages of this volume on which the work in question is mentioned. In the case of the Freud entries, the letters attached to the dates of publication are in accordance with the corresponding entries in the complete bibliography of Freud's writings to be included in the last volume of the *Standard Edition*.

For non-technical authors, and for technical authors where no specific work is mentioned, see the General Index.]

ABRAHAM, K. (1907) 'Das Erleiden sexueller Traumen als Form infantiler Sexualbetätigung', *Zbl. Nervenheilk. Psychiat.*, N.F. **18**, 854. (18)

[*Trans.*: 'The Experiencing of Sexual Traumas as a Form of Sexual Activity', *Selected Papers on Psycho-Analysis*, London, 1927, Chap. I.]

(1909) *Traum und Mythus: eine Studie zur Völkerpsychologie*, Leipzig and Vienna. (36)

[*Trans.*: 'Dreams and Myths: A Study in Folk-Psychology', *Clinical Papers and Essays on Psycho-Analysis*, London, 1955, Part III: Essays, 1.]

(1911) *Giovanni Segantini: ein psychoanalytischer Versuch*, Leipzig and Vienna. (37)

[*Trans.*: 'Giovanni Segantini: A Psycho-Analytical Study', *Clinical Papers and Essays on Psycho-Analysis*, London, 1955, Part III: Essays, 2.]

ADLER, A. (1907) *Studie über Minderwertigkeit von Organen*, Berlin and Vienna. (50–1, 56)

[*Trans.*: *Study of Organ-Inferiority and its Psychical Compensation*, New York, 1917.]

(1910) 'Der psychische Hermaphroditismus im Leben und in der Neurose', *Fortschr. Med.*, **28**, 486. (54)

(1911a) Review of C. G. Jung's 'Über Konflikte der kindlichen Seele' [*see* JUNG, C. G. (1910b)], *Zbl. Psychoan.*, **1**, 122. (56, 65)

(1911b) 'Beitrag zur Lehre vom Widerstand', *Zbl., Psychoan.*, **1**, 214. (57)

ADLER, A. (*cont.*)

(1912) *Über den nervösen Charakter*, Wiesbaden. (56–7)
[*Trans.*: *The Neurotic Constitution*, New York, 1916; London, 1918.]

(1914) With FURTMÜLLER, C. (eds.) *Heilen und Bilden*, Munich. (38)

BLEULER, E. (1906) *Affectivität, Suggestibilität, Paranoia, Halle.* (41)
[*Trans.*: *Affectivity, Suggestibility, Paranoia*, New York, 1912.]

(1910a) 'Die Psychanalyse Freuds', *Jb. psychoan. psychopath. Forsch.*, **2**, 623. (40–1)

(1911) *Dementia Praecox, oder Gruppe der Schizophrenien*, Leipzig and Vienna. (28–9)
[*Trans.*: *Dementia Praecox, or the Group of Schizophrenias*, New York, 1950.]

(1913) 'Kritik der Freudschen Theorien', *Allg. Z. Psychiat.*, **70**, 665. (41)

(1914) 'Die Kritiken der Schizophrenien', *Z. ges. Neurol. Psychiat.*, **22**, 19. (41)

BREUER, J., and FREUD, S.

(1895) *See* FREUD, S. (1895d)

BRILL, A. A. (1912) *Psychoanalysis: its Theories and Practical Application*, Philadelphia and London. (2nd ed., 1914; 3rd ed., 1922.) (32)

ELLIS, HAVELOCK

(1911) 'Die Lehren der Freud-Schule', *Zbl. Psychoan.*, **2**, 61. (30)

ERB, W. (1882) *Handbuch der Elektrotherapie*, Leipzig. (9)
[*Trans.*: *Handbook of Electro-Therapeutics*, London, 1883.]

FARROW, E. PICKWORTH (1926) 'Eine Kindheitserinnerung aus dem 6. Lebensmonat', *Int. Z. Psychoan.*, **12**, 79. (21)

FREUD, S. (1893f) 'Charcot', *G.S.*, **1**, 243; *G.W.*, **1**, 21. (22)
[*Trans.*: 'Charcot', *C.P.*, **1**, 9; *Standard Ed.*, **3**.]

(1894a) 'Die Abwehr-Neuropsychosen', *G.S.*, **1**, 290; *G.W.*, **1**, 59. (9.)
[*Trans.*: 'The Neuro-Psychoses of Defence', *C.P.*, **1**, 59; *Standard Ed.*, **3**.]

(1895d) With BREUER, J., *Studien über Hysterie*, Vienna. *G.S.*, **1**, 3; *G.W.*, **1**, 77 (omitting Breuer's contributions). (8–12, 29, 33)
[*Trans.*: *Studies on Hysteria, Standard Ed.*, **2**. Including Breuer's contributions.]

(1896b) 'Weitere Bemerkungen über die Abwehr-Neuropsychosen', *G.S.*, **1**, 363; *G.W.*, **1**, 379. (29)
[*Trans.*: 'Further Remarks on the Neuro-Psychoses of Defence', *C.P.*, **1**, 155; *Standard Ed.*, **3**.]

(1896c) 'Zur Atiologie der Hysterie', *G.S.*, **1**, 404; *G.W.*, **1**, 425. (21)
[*Trans.*:'The Aetiology of Hysteria', *C.P.*, **1**, 183; *Standard Ed.*, **3**.]

(1900a) *Die Traumdeutung*, Vienna. *G.S.*, **2–3**; *G.W.*, **2–3**. (19, 22, 23, 26, 28, 52, 57, 65)
[*Trans.*: *The Interpretation of Dreams*, London and New York, 1955; *Standard Ed.*, **4–5**.]

(1905c) *Der Witz und seine Beziehung zum Unbewussten,* Vienna. *G.S.,* **9,** 5; *G.W.,* **6.** (26, 37, 66)
[*Trans.: Jokes and their Relation to the Unconscious, Standard Ed.,* **8.**]

(1905d) *Drei Abhandlungen zur Sexualtheorie,* Vienna. *G.S.,* **5,** 3; *G.W.,* **5,** 29. (18, 55)
[*Trans.: Three Essays on the Theory of Sexuality,* London, 1949; *Standard Ed.,* **7,** 125.]

(1905e [1901]) 'Bruchstück einer Hysterie-Analyse', *G.S.,* **8,** 3; *G.W.,* **5,** 163. (10, 22)
[*Trans.:* 'Fragment of an Analysis of a Case of Hysteria', *C.P.,* **3,** 13; *Standard Ed.,* **7,** 3.]

(1906a) 'Meine Ansichten über die Rolle der Sexualität in der Ätiologie der Neurosen', *G.S.,* **5,** 123; *G.W.,* **5,** 149. (18)
[*Trans.:* 'My Views on the Part played by Sexuality in the Aetiology of the Neuroses', *C.P.,* **1,** 272; *Standard Ed.,* **7,** 271.]

(1906c) 'Tatbestandsdiagnostik und Psychoanalyse', *G.S.,* **10,** 197; *G.W.,* **7,** 3. (29)
[*Trans.:* 'Psycho-Analysis and the Establishment of the Facts in Legal Proceedings', *C.P.,* **2,** 13; *Standard Ed.,* **9.**]

(1907a) *Der Wahn und die Träume in W. Jensens 'Gradiva',* Vienna. *G.S.,* **9,** 273; *G.W.,* **7,** 31. (36)
[*Trans.: Delusions and Dreams in Jensen's 'Gradiva', Standard Ed.,* **9.**]

(1907b) 'Zwangshandlungen und Religionsübung', *G.S.,* **10,** 210; *G.W.,* **7,** 129. (37)
[*Trans.:* 'Obsessive Actions and Religious Practices', *C.P.,* **2,** 25; *Standard Ed.,* **9.**]

(1910a [1909]) *Über Psychoanalyse,* Vienna. *G.S.,* **4,** 349; *G.W.,* **8,** 3. (7, 31)
[*Trans.:* 'Five Lectures on Psycho-Analysis', *Amer. J. Psychol.,* **21** (1910), 181; *Standard Ed.,* **11,** 3.]

(1910c) *Eine Kindheitserinnerung des Leonardo da Vinci,* Vienna. *G.S.,* **9,** 371; *G.W.,* **8,** 128. (37)
[*Trans.: Leonardo da Vinci and a Memory of His Childhood, Standard Ed.,* **11,** 59.]

(1911g) Abstract of G. Greve's 'Sobre psicologia y psicoterapia de ciertos estados angustiosos', *Zbl. Psychoan.,* **1,** 594. (30)

(1912e) 'Ratschläge für den Arzt bei der psychoanalytischen Behandlung', *G.S.,* **6,** 64; *G.W.,* **8,** 376. (21)
[*Trans.:* 'Recommendations to Physicians Practising Psycho-Analysis', *C.P.,* **2,** 323; *Standard Ed.,* **12.**]

(1912-13) *Totem und Tabu,* Vienna, 1913, *G.S.,* **10,** 3; *G.W.,* **9.** (37)
[*Trans.: Totem and Taboo,* London, 1950; New York, 1952; *Standard Ed.,* **13,** 1.]

(1913b) Introduction to Pfister's *Die psychanalytische Methode, G.S.,* **11,** 224; *G.W.,* **10,** 448. (38)

FREUD, S. (*cont.*)
  [*Trans.: Standard Ed.*, **12**.]
  (1913*j*) 'Das Interesse an der Psychoanalyse', *G.S.*, **4**, 313; *G.W.*, **8**,
    390. (38)
    [*Trans.*: 'The Claims of Psycho-Analysis to Scientific Interest',
    Standard Ed., **13**, 165.]
  (1913*k*) Geleitwort zu J. G. Bourke, *Der Unrat in Sitte, Brauch,
    Glauben und Gewohnheitsrecht der Völker*, *G.S.*, **11**, 249; *G.W.*,
    10, 453. (13)
    [*Trans.*: 'Preface to J. G. Bourke's *Scatalogic Rites of all Nations*',
    C.P., **5**, 88; *Standard Ed.*, **12**.]
  (1913*m* [1911]) 'On Psycho-Analysis' [in English], *Aust. med. Congr.*
    (Transactions of the Ninth Session, held in Sydney, New South
    Wales, Sept. 1911), **2**, Part 8, 839; *Standard Ed.*, **12**. (30)
  (1914*c*) 'Zur Einführung des Narzissmus', *G.S.*, **6**, 155; *G.W.*,**10**,
    138. (4)
    [*Trans.*: 'On Narcissism: an Introduction', *C.P.* **4**, 30; *Standard
    Ed.*, **14**, 69.]
  (1915*d*) 'Die Verdrangung', *G.S.*, **5**, 466; *G.W.*, **10**, 248. (16)
    [*Trans.*: 'Repression', *C.P.*, **4**, 84; *Standard Ed.*, **14**, 143.]
    [*Trans.*: 'The Unconscious', *C.P.*, **4**, 98; *Standard Ed.*, **14**, 161.]
  (1916–17) *Vorlesungen zur Einführung in die Psychoanalyse,* Vienna.
    G.S., **7**; *G.W.*, **11**. (53)
    [*Trans.*: *Introductory Lectures on Psycho-Analysis*, revised ed.,
    London, 1929 (*A General Introduction to Psychoanalysis*, New
    York, 1935); *Standard Ed.*, **15–16**.]
  (1918*b* [1914]) 'Aus der Geschichte einer infantilen Neurose', *G.S.*,
    8, 439; *G.W.*, **12**, 29. (4, 56)
    [*Trans.*: 'From the History of an Infantile Neurosis', *C.P.*, **3**,
    473; *Standard Ed.*, **17**, 3.]
  (1919*b*) 'James J. Putnam', *G.S.*, **11**, 276; *G.W.*, **12**, 315. (32)
    [*Trans.*: 'James J. Putnam', *Standard Ed.*, **17**, 271.]
  (1919*c*) 'Internationaler psychoanalytischer Verlag und Preiszutei-
    lungen für psychoanalytische Arbeiten', *G.W.*, **12**, 333. (25)
    [*Trans.*: 'A Note on Psycho-Analytic Publications and Prizes',
    Standard Ed., **17**, 267.]
  (1919*e*) ' "Ein Kind wird geschlagen" ', *G.S.*, **5**, 344; *G.W.*, **12**,
    197. (5, 54)
    [*Trans.*: ' "A Child is Being Beaten" ', *C.P.*, **2**, 172; *Standard Ed.*,
    17, 177.]
  (1920*b*) 'Zur Vorgeschichte der analytischen Technik', *G.S.*, **6**, 148;
    G.W., **12**, 309. (16)
    [*Trans.*: 'A Note on the Prehistory of the Technique of Analysis',
    C.P., **5**, 101; *Standard Ed.*, **18**, 263.]
  (1921*a*) Preface [in English] to J. J. Putnam's *Addresses on Psycho-
    Analysis*, London and New York. *G.S.*, **11**, 262; *G.W.*, **13**, 437;
    Standard Ed., **18**, 269. (32)

(1923*b*) *Das Ich und das Es,* Vienna. *G.S.,* **6,** 353; *G.W.,* **13,** 237. (54)

[*Trans.: The Ego and the Id,* London, 1927; *Standard Ed.,* **19.**]

(1923*c*) 'Bemerkungen zur Theorie und Praxis der Traumdeutung', *G.S.,* **3,** 305; *G.W.,* **13,** 301. (65)

[*Trans.:* 'Remarks on the Theory and Practice of Dream-Interpretation', *C.P.,* **5,** 136; *Standard Ed.,* **19.**]

(1923*f*) 'Josef Popper-Lynkeus und die Theorie des Traumes', *G.S.,* **11,** 295; *G.W.,* **13,** 357. (20)

[*Trans.:* 'Josef Popper-Lynkeus and the Theory of Dreams', *Standard Ed.,* **19.**]

(1923*g*) Preface to Max Eitingon's *Bericht über die Berliner Psychoanalytische Poliklinik,* Vienna. *G.S.,* **11,** 265; *G.W.,* **13,** 441. (26)

[*Trans.:* Preface to Eitingon's Report on the Berlin Psycho-Analytical Clinic, *Standard Ed.,* **19.**]

(1923*i*) 'Dr. Ferenczi Sándor', *G.S.,* **11,** 273; *G.W.,* **13,** 443. (34)

[*Trans.:* 'Dr. Sándor Ferenczi on his Fiftieth Birthday', *Standard Ed.,* **19.**]

(1925*d* [1924]) *Selbstdarstellung,* Vienna, 1934. *G.S.,* **11,** 119; *G.W.,* **14,** 33. (5, 23)

[*Trans.: An Autobiographical Study,* London, 1935 *(Autobiography,* New York 1935); *Standard Ed.,* **20.**]

(1925*j*) 'Einige psychische Folgen des anatomischen Geschlechtsunterschieds', *G.S.,* **11,** 8; *G.W.,* **14,** 19. (55)

[*Trans.:* 'Some Psychological Consequences of the Anatomical Distinction between the Sexes', *C.P.,* **5,** 186; *Standard Ed.,* **19.**]

(1926*c*) Note on E. Pickworth Farrow's 'Eine Kindheitserinnerung aus dem 6. Lebensmonat', *G.W.,* **14,** 568 (21)

[*Trans.:* 'Foreword' to E. Pickworth Farrow's *A Practical Method of Self-Analysis,* London, 1942; *Standard Ed.,* **20.**]

(1926*d*) *Hemmung, Symptom und Angst,* Vienna. *G.S.,* **11,** 23; *G.W.,* **14,** 113. (11)

[*Trans.: Inhibitions, Symptoms and Anxiety,* London, 1936 (*The Problem of Anxiety,* New York, 1936); *Standard Ed.,* **20.**]

(1930*b*) Preface to *Zehn Jahre Berliner Psychoanalytisches Institut,* Vienna. *G.S.,* **12,** 388; *G.W.,* **14,** 572. (26)

[*Trans.:* In 'Personal Memories', in *Max Eitingon In Memoriam,* Jerusalem; *Standard Ed.,* **21.**]

(1932*c*) 'Meine Berührung mit Josef Popper-Lynkeus', *G.S.,* **12,** 415; *G.W.,* **16,** 261. (20)

[*Trans.:* 'My Contact with Josef Popper-Lynkeus', *C.P.,* **5,** 295; *Standard Ed.,* **22.**]

(1935*b*) 'Die Feinheit einer Fehlhandlung', *G.W.,* **16,** 37. (21)

[*Trans.:* 'The Subtleties of a Faulty Action', *C.P.,* **5,** 313; *Standard Ed.,* **22.**]

(1937*c*) 'Die endliche und die unendliche Analyse', *G.W.,* **16,** 59. (21)

FREUD, S. (*cont.*)

    [*Trans.:* 'Analysis Terminable and Interminable', *C.P.*, **5**, 316; *Standard Ed.*, **23**.]

    (1950*a* [1887–1902]) *Aus den Anfängen der Psychoanalyse,* London. Includes 'Entwurf einer Psychologie' (1895). (7, 18, 20, 42)

    [*Trans.: The Origins of Psycho-Analysis,* London and New York, 1954. (Partly, including 'A Project for a Scientific Psychology', in *Standard Ed.,* **1.**)]

    (1956*a*) [1886] 'Report on my Studies in Paris and Berlin, carried out with the assistance of a Travelling Bursary Granted from the University Jubilee Fund, 1885–6', *Int. J. Psycho-Anal.,* **37**, 2; *Standard Ed.,* **1.** (9, 13)

    [*German Text:* 'Bericht über meine mit Universitäts-Jubiläums Reisestipendium unternommene Studienreise nach Paris und Berlin', in Gicklhorn's *Sigmund Freuds Akademische Laufbahn,* Vienna, 1960.]

FURTMÜLLER, C., and ADLER, A. (1914) *See* ADLER, A. (1914)

GREVE, G. (1910) 'Sobre Psicologia y Psicoterapia de ciertos estados angustiosos', Lecture to Neurological Section of the Int. American Congress of Medicine and Hygiene, Buenos Aires. (30)

HESNARD, A., and RÉGIS, E. (1914) *See* RÉGIS, E., and HESNARD, A. (1914)

HOCHE, A. (1910) 'Eine psychische Epidemie unter Ärzten', *Med. Klin.,* **6**, 1007. (27)

HUG-HELLMUTH, H. VON (1913) *Aus dem Seelenleben des Kindes,* Leipzig and Vienna. (38)

    [*Trans.: A Study of the Mental Life of the Child,* New York, 1919.]

JANET, PIERRE (1913) 'Psycho-Analysis. Rapport par M. le Dr. Pierre Janet', *Int. Congr. Med.,* **17**, Section XII (Psychiatry) (1), 13. (32–3, 39)

JELGERSMA, G. (1914) *Ongeweten Geestesleven,* Leyden. (33)

    [*German Trans.: Unbewusstes Geistesleben, Beiheft der Int. Z. Psychoan.,* I, Leipzig and Vienna, 1914.]

JONES, ERNEST (1908) 'Rationalization in Everyday Life', *J. Abnorm. Psychol.,* **3**, 161. (52)

    (1910) 'On the Nightmare', *Amer. J. Insanity,* **66**, 383. Revised and enlarged ed., in book form, London, 1931. (36)

    (1912) 'Die Bedeutung des Salzes in Sitte und Brauch der Völker', *Imago,* **1**, 361, 454. (36)

    [*English Text:* 'The Symbolic Significance of Salt in Folklore and Superstition' *Essays in Applied Psycho-Analysis,* **2**, London, 1951.]

    (1913) *Papers on Psycho-Analysis,* London and New York. (2nd ed., 1918; 3rd ed., 1923; 4th ed., 1938; 5th ed., 1948.) (32)

    (1915) 'Professor Janet on Psychoanalysis: a Rejoinder', *J. abnorm. (soc.) Psychol.,* **9**, 400. (33)

    [*German Trans.:* 'Professor Janet über Psychoanalyse', *Int. Z. (ärztl.) Psychoanal.,* **4** (1916), 34.]

(1953) *Sigmund Freud: Life and Work*, Vol. 1, London and New York. (5, 12, 16)

(1955) *Sigmund Freud: Life and Work*, Vol. 2, London and New York. (3, 5)

(1957) *Sigmund Freud: Life and Work*, Vol. 3, London and New York. (5)

(N.B. Page references in the above three items are to the *London* editions.)

JUNG, C. G. (1902) *Zur Psychologie und Pathologie sogenannter okkulter Phänomene*, Leipzig. (28)

[*Trans.*: 'On the Psychology and Pathology of So-called Occult Phenomena', *Collected Papers on Analytical Psychology*, London, 1916, Chap. I.]

(1906) (ed.) *Diagnostische Assoziationsstudien*, Leipzig. (29)
[*Trans.*: *Studies in Word-Association*, London, 1918.]

(1907) *Über die Psychologie der Dementia praecox*, Halle. (28–9)
[*Trans.*: *The Psychology of Dementia Praecox*, New York, 1909.]

(1910*a*) 'The Association Method', *Amer. J. Psychol.*, **21**, 219 (31)

(1910*b*) 'Experiences Concerning the Psychic Life of the Child', *Amer. J. Psychol.*, **21**, 251. (31, 65)

(1910*c*) 'Uber Konflikte der kindlichen Seele', *Jb. psychoan. psychopath. Forsch.*, **2**, 33. [A slightly different version of 1910*b*.] (56)

(1912) *Wandlungen und Symbole der Libido*, Leipzig and Vienna. (29)
[*Trans.*: *Psychology of the Unconscious*, New York, 1916; London, 1919.]

(1913) *Versuch einer Darstellung der psychoanalytischen Theorie*, Leipzig and Vienna. (66)
[*Trans.*: *The Theory of Psychoanalysis*, New York, 1915.]

MAEDER, A. (1912) 'Über die Funktion des Traumes', *Jb. psychoan. psychopath. Forsch.*, **4**, 692. (57)

NELKEN, J. (1912) 'Analytische Beobachtungen über Phantasien eines Schizophrenen', *Jb. psychoan. psychopath. Forsch.*, **4**, 504. (36)

PFISTER, O. (1910) *Die Frömmigkeit des Grafen Ludwig von Zinzendorf*, Leipzig and Vienna. (37)

(1913) *Die psychanalytische Methode*, Leipzig and Berlin. (38)
[*Trans.*: *The Psychoanalytic Method*, New York and London, 1917.]

POPPER, J. ('LYNKEUS') (1899) *Phantasien eines Realisten*, Dresden. (16, 20)

PUTNAM, J. J. (1912) 'Über die Bedeutung philosophischer Anschauungen und Ausbildung für die weitere Entwickelung der psychoanalytischen Bewegung', *Imago*, **1**, 101. (45)
[*English Text*: 'A Plea for the Study of Philosophic Methods in Preparation for Psychoanalytic Work', *Addresses on Psycho-Analysis*, London, Vienna and New York, 1921, Chap. IV.]

(1921) *Addresses on Psycho-Analysis*, London, Vienna and New York. (32)

RANK, O. (1907) *Der Künstler*, Vienna. (36)
   (1909) *Der Mythus von der Geburt des Helden*, Leipzig and Vienna. (36)
   [*Trans.: The Myth of the Birth of the Hero*, New York, 1914.]
   (1911a) 'Schopenhauer über den Wahnsinn', *Zbl. Psychoan.*, **1**, 69. (15)
   (1911b) *Die Lohengrinsage*, Leipzig and Vienna. (36)
   (1912) *Das Inzest-Motiv in Dichtung und Sage*, Leipzig and Vienna. (37)
   (1913) With SACHS, H., *Die Bedeutung der Psychoanalyse für die Geisteswissenschaften*, Wiesbaden. (35)
   [*Trans.: The Significance of Psychoanalysis for the Mental Sciences*, New York, 1916.]
RÉGIS, E., and HESNARD, A. (1914) *La Psychoanalyse des Névroses et des Psychoses*, Paris. (32)
REIK, T. (1912) *Flaubert und seine 'Versuchung des heiligen Antonius'*, Minden. (36)
RENTERGHEM, A. W. VAN (1913) *Freud en zijn School*, Baarn. (33)
RIKLIN, F. (1908) *Wunscherfüllung und Symbolik im Märchen*, Leipzig and Vienna. (36)
   [*Trans.: Wishfulfillment and Symbolism in Fairy Tales*, New York, 1915: "by F. Ricklin".]
SACHS, H., and RANK, O. (1913) *See* RANK, O. (1913)
SADGER, I. (1909) *Aus dem Liebesleben Nicolaus Lenaus*, Leipzig and Vienna. (36)
SCHERNER, K. A. (1861) *Das Leben des Traumes*, Berlin. (19)
STORFER, A. J. (1914) *Marias jungfräuliche Mutterschaft*, Berlin. (36)
VOGT, R. (1907) *Psykiatriens grundtraek*, Christiania. (33)

LIST OF ABBREVIATIONS

G.S. = Freud, *Gesammelte Schriften* (12 vols.), Vienna, 1924–34
G.W. = Freud, *Gesammelte Werke* (18 vols.), London, from 1940
C.P. = Freud, *Collected Papers* (5 vols.), London, 1924–50
Standard Ed. = Freud, *Standard Edition* (24 vols.), London, from 1953

GENERAL INDEX

This index includes the names of non-technical authors. It also includes the names of technical authors where no reference is made in the text to specific works. For references to specific technical works, the Bibliography should be consulted.

NORTON BOOKS
in Psychiatry and Psychology

GROTJAHN, MARTIN
Psychoanalysis and the Family Neurosis

HORNEY, KAREN
Feminine Psychology
Neurosis and Human Growth
The Neurotic Personality of our Time
New Ways in Psychoanalysis
Our Inner Conflicts
Self-Analysis

HORNEY, KAREN, ED.
Are You Considering Psychoanalysis?

KELLY, GEORGE A.
The Psychology of Personal Constructs, 2 Volumes

KELMAN, HAROLD, ED.
Advances in Psychoanalysis
New Perspectives in Psychoanalysis

LEWIN, BERTRAM D. and ROSS, HELEN
Psychoanalytic Education in the United States

LIFTON, ROBERT JAY
Thought Reform and the Psychology of Totalism

MAY, ROLLO
Man's Search for Himself

PEARSON, G. H. J.
Adolescence and the Conflict of Generations
Emotional Disorders of Children

ROSE, ARNOLD, ED.
Mental Health and Mental Disorder

RUESCH, JURGEN
Disturbed Communication
Therapeutic Communication

RUESCH, JURGEN and BATESON, GREGORY
Communication

SCHILDER, PAUL
Psychotherapy

SULLIVAN, HARRY STACK
Clinical Studies in Psychiatry
Conceptions of Modern Psychiatry
The Interpersonal Theory of Psychiatry
The Fusion of Psychiatry and Social Science
The Psychiatric Interview
Schizophrenia as a Human Process

VAN DEN BERG, J. H.
  The Changing Nature of Man

WALTER, W. GREY
  The Living Brain

WATZLAWICK, PAUL; BEAVIN, JANET; and
  JACKSON, DON D.
  Pragmatics of Human Communication

WHEELIS, ALLEN
  The Quest for Identity

WYSS, DIETER
  Depth Psychology

ZILBOORG, GREGORY and HENRY, GEORGE W.
  History of Medical Psychology

Norton Paperbacks on Psychiatry and Psychology

Abraham, Karl. *On Character and Libido Development, Six Essays,* edited by Bertram D. Lewin, M.D.

Alexander, Franz. *Fundamentals of Psychoanalysis.*

Alexander, Franz. *Psychosomatic Medicine.*

Brill, A. A. *Freud's Contribution to Psychiatry.*

Cannon, Walter B. *The Wisdom of the Body.*

Erikson, Erik H. *Childhood and Society.*

Erikson, Erik H. *Insight and Responsibility.*

Erikson, Erik H. *Young Man Luther.*

Freud, Sigmund. *An Autobiographical Study.*

Freud, Sigmund. *Civilization and its Discontents.*

Freud, Sigmund. *The Ego and the Id.*

Freud, Sigmund. *Jokes and Their Relation to the Unconscious.*

Freud, Sigmund. *Leonardo da Vinci and a Memory of His Childhood.*

Freud, Sigmund. *New Introductory Lectures on Psychoanalysis.*

Freud, Sigmund. *On Dreams.*

Freud, Sigmund. *An Outline of Psychoanalysis.*

Freud, Sigmund. *The Problem of Anxiety.*

Freud, Sigmund. *The Psychopathology of Everyday Life.*

Freud, Sigmund. *Totem and Taboo.*

Hinsie, Leland E. *The Person in the Body.*

Horney, Karen. *Are You Considering Psychoanalysis?*

Horney, Karen. *New Ways in Psychoanalysis.*

Horney, Karen. *The Neurotic Personality of Our Time.*

Horney, Karen. *Our Inner Conflicts.*

James, William. *Talks to Teachers.*

Kasanin, J. S. *Language and Thought in Schizophrenia.*

Kelly, George A. *A Theory of Personality.*

Klein, Melanie and Riviere, Joan. *Love, Hate and Reparation.*

Levy, David M. *Maternal Overprotection.*

Lifton, Robert Jay. *Thought Reform and the Psychology of Totalism.*

Piaget, Jean. *The Child's Conception of Number.*

Piaget, Jean. *The Origins of Intelligence in Childhood.*

Piaget, Jean. *Play, Dreams and Imitation in Childhood.*

Sullivan, Harry Stack. *Conceptions of Modern Psychiatry.*

Wheelis, Allen. *The Quest for Identity.*

Zilboorg, Gregory. *A History of Medical Psychology.*